MODERN BRITISH SOCIETY: A BIBLIOGRAPHY

John Westergaard

Anne Weyman

Paul Wiles

Frances Pinter (Publishers) Ltd

Published by

Frances Pinter (Publishers) Ltd
161 West End Lane London NW6 2LG

First published 1974
ISBN 0 903804 07 7

MODERN BRITISH SOCIETY : A BIBLIOGRAPHY

Introduction

This bibliography is intended as a fairly detailed guide to the literature and research on contemporary British social structure and its immediate historical background.

It is an up-dated and extensively revised version of successive bibliographies on the same subject, produced over a number of years by members of the teaching staff of the Department of Sociology at the London School of Economics, and circulated there for internal use by students of the LSE. We should like to acknowledge the contributions made by colleagues there, associated over the years with the teaching of the Social Structure of Modern Britain — especially Michael Burrage, Charlotte Erickson, David Glass, Alan Little, Bob McKenzie and Asher Tropp — to earlier unpublished versions. We also wish to thank Mike Hill for his help with one section of the present published version; and Sheila Green and Greta Johnson for their secretarial assistance.

Literature and research in this field have grown to very large dimensions, in recent years especially. The bibliography is, therefore, inevitably selective; and we have felt compelled, in particular, to keep references to journal articles to a minimum in order to give manageable proportions to the bibliography.

The present edition is up-to-date to the spring of 1974, as far as practicable, with some forthcoming titles included. We hope that it may be possible to produce further editions, possibly through the publication of supplements.

John Westergaard
Anne Weyman
Paul Wiles

Introduction

This bibliography is intended as a fairly detailed guide to the literature and research on contemporary British social structure and its
immediate historical background.

It is an up-dated and extensively revised version of successive bibliographies on the same subject, produced over a number of years by members
of the teaching staff of the Department of Sociology at the London School
of Economics, and circulated there for internal use by students of the
LSE. We should like to acknowledge the contributions made by colleagues
there, associated over the years with the teaching of the Social Structure
of Modern Britain – especially Michael Burrage, Charlotte Erickson,
David Glass, Alan Little, Bob McKenzie and Asher Tropp – to earlier
unpublished versions. We also wish to thank Mike Hill for his help with
one section of the present published version; and Sheila Green and Greta
Johnson for their secretarial assistance.

Literature and research in this field have grown to very large dimensions,
in recent years especially. The bibliography is, therefore, inevitably
selective; and we have felt compelled, in particular, to keep references
to journal articles to a minimum in order to give manageable proportions
to the bibliography.

The present edition is up-to-date to the spring of 1974, as far as
practicable, with some forthcoming titles included. We hope that it may
be possible to produce further editions, possibly through the publication
of supplements.

John Westergaard
Anne Weyman
Paul Wiles

MODERN BRITISH SOCIETY : CLASSIFICATION

A GENERAL

Bailey R U and Young J eds — CONTEMPORARY SOCIAL PROBLEMS IN BRITAIN Saxon House Farnborough 1973

Banks J A ed — STUDIES IN BRITISH SOCIETY Routledge and Kegan Paul London 1969

Butterworth E and Weir D eds — SOCIAL PROBLEMS OF MODERN BRITAIN Fontana London 1972

Butterworth E and Weir D eds — THE SOCIOLOGY OF MODERN BRITAIN Fontana/Collins London 1970

Carr-Saunders A et al — A SURVEY OF SOCIAL CONDITIONS IN ENGLAND AND WALES Oxford University Press London 1958

Cotgrove S — THE SCIENCE OF SOCIETY: AN INTRODUCTION TO SOCIOLOGY Allen and Unwin London (revised edition 1973)

Ginsberg M ed — LAW AND OPINION IN ENGLAND IN THE 20TH CENTURY Stevens London 1959

Glass D V — NUMBERING THE PEOPLE Gregg International London 1973

Krausz E — SOCIOLOGY IN BRITAIN: A SURVEY OF RESEARCH Batsford London 1969

Rex John ed — APPROACHES TO SOCIOLOGY Routledge and Kegan Paul London 1974

Ryder Judith and Silver Harold — MODERN ENGLISH SOCIETY: HISTORY AND STRUCTURE 1850-1970 Methuen London 1970

Swann Brenda and Turnbull Maureen — RECORDS OF INTEREST TO SOCIAL SCIENTISTS 1919-1939 Public Record Office Handbooks no 14 HMSO London 1971

United Kingdom: Central Statistical Office — SOCIAL TRENDS Annually since 1970 HMSO London

United Kingdom Office of Population Censuses and Surveys — GENERAL HOUSEHOLD SURVEY: INTRODUCTORY REPORT HMSO London 1973

Welford A T et al ed — SOCIETY Routledge and Kegan Paul London 1962

B   HISTORICAL INTRODUCTION
(see also under relevant subject headings)

B 10 General Historical Background

Black Eugene C ed	BRITISH POLITICS IN THE NINETEENTH CENTURY Macmillan London 1970
Branson Noreen and Heinemann Margot	BRITAIN IN THE NINETEEN THIRTIES Weidenfeld and Nicolson London 1971
Briggs A	THE AGE OF IMPROVEMENT 1780-1867 Longman London 1959
Burn T and Saul S B eds	SOCIAL THEORY AND ECONOMIC CHANGE by Michael Argyle and others Tavistock Publications 1967 Seminar on the Theory of Economic Change Edinburgh University 1965
Calder A	THE PEOPLE'S WAR: BRITAIN 1939-45 Cape London 1969
Clark G K	THE MAKING OF VICTORIAN ENGLAND Methuen London 1962
Cole G D H and Postgate R W	THE COMMON PEOPLE 1746-1938 Methuen London 1961 (1st ed 1938)
Court W H B	A CONCISE ECONOMIC HISTORY OF BRITAIN FROM 1750 TO RECENT TIMES Book II Cambridge University Press London 1954
Dangerfield G	THE STRANGE DEATH OF LIBERAL ENGLAND Paladin London 1970 (1st ed 1935)
Ensor R C K	ENGLAND 1870-1914 (The Oxford History of England) Oxford University Press London 1936 (Chapters 4 5 9 10 14 and 15)
Foster John	CLASS STRUGGLE AND THE INDUSTRIAL REVOLUTION Weidenfeld and Nicolson London 1974
Halevy E	HISTORY OF THE ENGLISH PEOPLE IN THE NINE- TEENTH CENTURY Vol V: IMPERIALISM AND THE RISE OF LABOUR Benn 1929 Vol VI: THE RULE OF DEMO- CRACY 1905-14 Benn London 1934
Harrison J F C	ROBERT OWEN AND THE OWENITES IN BRITAIN AND AMERICA: THE QUEST FOR THE NEW MORAL ORDER Routledge and Kegan Paul London 1969
Hobsbawm E J	THE AGE OF REVOLUTION: 1789-1848 Weidenfeld and Nicolson London 1962

Hobsbawm E J   INDUSTRY AND EMPIRE Weidenfeld and Nicolson
                      London 1968

Hobsbawm E J   LABOURING MEN Weidenfeld and Nicolson London
                      1964

Kiernan E V G   THE LORDS OF HUMAN KIND Little

Mowat C L   BRITAIN BETWEEN THE WARS 1918–1940 Methuen
                      London 1955 (Chapters 4 and 9)

Neale R S   CLASS AND IDEOLOGY IN THE NINETEENTH CENTURY
                      Routledge and Kegan Paul London 1972

Perkin H   THE ORIGINS OF MODERN ENGLISH SOCIETY: 1780–
                      1880 Routledge and Kegan Paul London 1969

Radzinowicz L   HISTORY OF THE ENGLISH CRIMINAL LAW 4 vols
                      Stevens and Sons London 1948–1969

Royston Pike E   HUMAN DOCUMENTS IN THE AGE OF THE FORSYTES
                      Allen and Unwin London 1970

Thompson E P   THE MAKING OF THE ENGLISH WORKING CLASS
                      Gollancz London 1963 (Revised Pelican edition
                      1968)

Young G M   EARLY VICTORIAN ENGLAND Oxford University Press
                      London 1934 (Chapters 1–4 and 17)

Young G M   VICTORIAN ENGLAND: PORTRAIT OF AN AGE Oxford
                      University Press London 1961 (1st ed 1937)

B 20 Social Conditions in the Mid-Nineteenth Century

B 20 General

Engels F and Marx K   ON BRITAIN Foreign Language Publishing House
                      Moscow 1953

Giffen R   'The progress of the working classes in the last
                      half century'; 'Further notes on the progress
                      of the working classes' ESSAYS IN FINANCE 2nd
                      series 1886

Hammond J L and B   THE BLEAK AGE Longmans Toronto 1947 (1st ed
                      1934)

Poor Law Commission   REPORT OF THE SANITARY CONDITION OF THE
                      LABOURING POPULATION OF GREAT BRITAIN House
                      of Lords Sessional Papers 1842 vols XXVI–XXVIII
                      (1965 edition edited and introduced by M W Flinn)

Ingestre V ed Talbot C H C	MELIORA, OR BETTER TIMES TO COME 1852
Laing S	NATIONAL DISTRESS: ITS CAUSES AND REMEDIES (Atlas: The Prize Essays) 1844
Local Government Board	STATISTICAL MEMORANDA AND DATA... RELATING TO PUBLIC HEALTH AND SOCIAL CONDITIONS 1909
Ludlow J M and Jones L I	PROGRESS OF THE WORKING CLASS 1832-67 1867
Royal Sanitary Commission	FIRST REPORT, WITH MINUTES OF EVIDENCE 1870; British Parliamentary Papers 1868-9 XXXII SECOND REPORT, MINUTES OF EVIDENCE 1871 and 1874 3 vols; British Parliamentary Papers 1871 XXXV, 1873 XXXI
Simon J	PUBLIC HEALTH REPORTS 2 Vols 1887
Taylor W C	NOTES OF A TOUR IN THE MANUFACTURING DISTRICTS OF LANCASHIRE Frank Cass London (2nd ed 1842)
Tobias J J	CRIME AND INDUSTRIAL SOCIETY IN THE NINETEENTH CENTURY Batsford/Penguin Harmondsworth 1972
Wright T	(The Journeyman Engineer) THE GREAT UNWASHED 1868

B 21 In towns and cities

Ashworth W	THE GENESIS OF MODERN BRITISH TOWN PLANNING Routledge and Kegan Paul London 1954 (Chapters 2-4)
Briggs A	VICTORIAN CITIES Odhams London 1963
Dyos H J	VICTORIAN SUBURB: A STUDY OF THE GROWTH OF CAMBERWELL Leicester University Press Leicester 1961
Godwin G	TOWN SWAMPS AND SOCIAL BRIDGES 1859
Jones Gareth Stedman	OUTCAST LONDON Clarendon Press London 1971 See also: Kiernan Victor 'Victorian London: Unending Purgatory' New Left Review 76 Nov/Dec 1972
Mayhew H	LONDON LABOUR AND THE LONDON POOR 1861-62 4 vols Frank Cass London 1967/Dover Publications London 1969
Read D	THE ENGLISH PROVINCES ca 1760-1960 Edward Arnold London 1964
Roberts Robert	THE CLASSIC SLUM: SALFORD LIFE IN THE FIRST QUARTER OF THE CENTURY Manchester University Press Manchester 1971

Simey T S and M B   CHARLES BOOTH: SOCIAL SCIENTIST Oxford University Press London 1960

Thompson E P and Yeo E   THE UNKNOWN MAYHEW Merlin London 1971

United Kingdom   THE COMMISSIONERS FOR INQUIRING INTO THE STATE OF LARGE TOWNS AND POPULOUS DISTRICTS FOR REPORT AND MINUTES OF EVIDENCE 1840
British Parliamentary Papers 1844 XVII
SECOND REPORT AND MINUTES OF EVIDENCE 1845
British Parliamentary Paper 1845 XVIII

Weber A F   THE GROWTH OF CITIES IN THE NINETEENTH CENTURY (1899) Cornell University Press Ithaca New York 1963

B 22 In rural places

Chambers J D and Mingay G E THE AGRICULTURAL REVOLUTION 1750-1880 Batsford London 1966

Hasbach W   HISTORY OF THE ENGLISH AGRICULTURAL LABOURER 1908 Frank Cass London 1966

Russell H A   11th Duke of Bedford: A GREAT AGRICULTURAL ESTATE 1897

Saville J   RURAL DEPOPULATION IN ENGLAND AND WALES 1851-1951 Routledge and Kegan Paul London 1957

Springall L M   LABOURING LIFE IN NORFOLK VILLAGES 1834-1914 George Allen London 1936

Thompson F M L   ENGLISH LANDED SOCIETY IN THE NINETEENTH CENTURY Routledge and Kegan Paul London 1963/1971

B 30 Social Structure in the mid-nineteenth century

B 30 General

Annan N G   'The intellectual aristocracy' in J H Plumb ed: STUDIES IN SOCIAL HISTORY Longmans London 1955

Briggs A ed   CHARTIST STUDIES Macmillan London 1959

Briggs A   'Social structure and politics in Birmingham and Lyons 1825-1848' British Journal of Sociology 1 (1) March 1950

Briggs A   VICTORIAN PEOPLE... 1857-1867 Penguin Harmondsworth 1954

Escott T H S   ENGLAND: ITS PEOPLE, POLITY AND PURSUITS New edition 1885

Escott T H S   SOCIAL TRANSFORMATIONS OF THE VICTORIAN AGE
                                      1897

Farr W   VITAL STATISTICS (Ed Humphreys N A) 1885

Guttsman W L ed   THE ENGLISH RULING CLASS Weidenfeld and
                                      Nicolson London 1969

Lewis R and Maude A E U   THE ENGLISH MIDDLE CLASSES Phoenix House London
                                      1949

Murray E C G   SIDELIGHTS ON ENGLISH SOCIETY, OR SKETCHES
                                      FROM LIFE, SOCIAL AND SATIRICAL 1881 (2 Vols)

Osborne S G   THE LETTERS OF S G O: A SERIES OF LETTERS PUB-
                                      LISHED IN 'THE TIMES' 1890 (2 Vols)

B 31   Occupations

Booth C   OCCUPATIONS OF THE PEOPLE: ENGLAND, SCOTLAND,
                                      IRELAND 1841-1881   1886

Carr-Saunders A M and   THE PROFESSIONS Oxford University Press London
Wilson P A   1933

Day C   THE DISTRIBUTION OF INDUSTRIAL OCCUPATIONS IN
                                      ENGLAND 1841-1861 (Connecticut Academy of
                                      Arts and Sciences, Transactions Vol 28) 1927

Erickson C J   BRITISH INDUSTRIALISTS: STEEL AND HOSIERY
                                      1850-1950 Cambridge University Press London
                                      1959

Hewitt M   WIVES AND MOTHERS IN VICTORIAN INDUSTRY
                                      Rockliffe London 1958

Pinchbeck I   WOMEN WORKERS AND THE INDUSTRIAL REVOLUTION
                                      1750-1850 Frank Cass London 1930

Reader W J   PROFESSIONAL MEN: THE RISE OF THE PROFESSIONAL
                                      CLASSES IN NINETEENTH CENTURY ENGLAND Weiden-
                                      feld and Nicolson London 1966

Spackman W F   ANALYSIS OF THE OCCUPATIONS OF THE PEOPLE OF
                                      THE UNITED KINGDOM 1847

B 32   Income and wealth

Baxter R D   NATIONAL INCOME: THE UNITED KINGDOM... READ
                                      BEFORE THE STATISTICAL SOCIETY OF LONDON 1868

Bowley A L   WAGES AND INCOME IN THE UNITED KINGDOM SINCE
                                      1860 Cambridge University Press London 1937

Pollard S and Crossley D W   THE WEALTH OF BRITAIN 1885-1966 Batsford London 1968

Thompson T M L   ENGLISH LANDED SOCIETY IN THE NINETEENTH CEN-TURY Routledge and Kegan Paul London 1963

see also: Mingay G E ENGLISH LANDED SOCIETY IN THE EIGHTEENTH CENTURY Routledge and Kegan Paul London 1963

Wood G H   'Real wages and the standard of comfort since 1850' Journal of the Royal Statistical Society 1909 Vol LXXII

B 40   Social Institutions in the mid-nineteenth century

B 40   Education and schools

Altick R D   THE ENGLISH COMMON READER... 1800-1900 University of Chicago Press Chicago and London 1957

Arnold M   REPORTS ON ELEMENTARY SCHOOLS 1852-82   1889

Harrison J F C   LEARNING AND LIVING 1790-1960 Routledge and Kegan Paul London 1961

Musgrove F   'Middle class education and employment in the Nineteenth century' Economic History Review August 1959

see also critique by Perkin H J Economic History Review August 1961

Report of the Royal Commission on Popular Education   BRITISH PARLIAMENTARY PAPER 1861 Vol XXI

Rothblatt S   THE REVOLUTION OF THE DONS: CAMBRIDGE AND SOCIETY IN VICTORIAN ENGLAND Faber London 1968

Tylecote M   MECHANICS INSTITUTES OF LANCASHIRE AND YORK-SHIRE BEFORE 1851 Manchester University Press Manchester 1957

Webb R K   THE BRITISH WORKING CLASS READER 1790-1848 George Allen London 1955

B 41 Religion and churches

Beck G A   THE ENGLISH CATHOLICS 1850-1950 (Chapters 1 and 2) Burns London 1950

Cornish F W   THE ENGLISH CHURCH IN THE NINETEENTH CENTURY 2 vols London 1910

| Cowherd R G | POLITICS OF ENGLISH DISSENT 1815-48 New York University Press New York 1956 |

| Inglis K S | CHURCHES AND THE WORKING CLASSES IN VICTORIAN ENGLAND Routledge and Kegan Paul London 1963 |

| Maclaren A Allan | RELIGION AND SOCIAL CLASS: THE DISRUPTION YEARS IN ABERDEEN Routledge and Kegan Paul London 1974 |

| Semmel Bernard | THE METHODIST REVOLUTION Heinemann London 1974 |

| United Kingdom | CENSUS OF GREAT BRITAIN 1851: RELIGIOUS WORSHIP, ENGLAND AND WALES 1853 British Parliamentary Papers 1852-3 LXXXIX |

B 42   Working class organisations

| Baernreither J M | ENGLISH ASSOCIATIONS OF WORKING MEN (Translated by A Taylor) 1893 |

| Briggs A and Saville J eds | ESSAYS IN LABOUR HISTORY (Chapters 1-3 and 9) Macmillan London 1960 |

| Brown E H P | THE GROWTH OF BRITISH INDUSTRIAL RELATIONS (Chapters 1-3) Macmillan London 1959 |

| Cole G D H | 'British trade unions in the third quarter of the Nineteenth Century' International Review of Social History Leiden 1937 Vol II |

| National Association for the Promotion of Social Science | Committee on Trade Societies and Strikes: REPORT ON TRADE SOCIETIES AND STRIKES 1860 |

| Potter B | THE COOPERATIVE MOVEMENT IN GREAT BRITAIN 1891 |

| Thompson E P | THE MAKING OF THE ENGLISH WORKING CLASS Penguin Harmondsworth 1963 |

| Webb S and B | THE HISTORY OF TRADE UNIONISM 1866-1920 Longman London 4th ed 1950 (1st ed 1920) |

B 43 Social policy

| Beales H L | THE MAKING OF SOCIAL POLICY Oxford University Press London 1945 |

| Brebner J B | 'Laissez faire and state intervention in 19th century Britain' Journal of Economic History Supplement VIII 1948 |

| Butt J and Clarke I F eds | THE VICTORIANS AND SOCIAL PROTEST David and Charles Newton Abbot 1973 |

| Gray B K | PHILANTHROPY AND THE STATE P S King and Son London 1908 |

| Roberts D | THE VICTORIAN ORIGINS OF THE BRITISH WELFARE STATE Oxford University Press London 1960 |

C CLASS STRUCTURE

C 10 General

Abrams M A — THE CONDITION OF THE BRITISH PEOPLE 1911-1945 Gollancz London 1946

Anderson P — 'Origins of the present crisis' in Anderson P and Blackburn R eds TOWARDS SOCIALISM Fontana Library London 1965

Barber B and E G eds — EUROPEAN SOCIAL CLASS: STABILITY AND CHANGE Macmillan New York 1965

Bendix R and Lipset S M eds — CLASS, STATUS AND POWER Part 1 Routledge and Kegan Paul London 1954 Glencoe Free Press Illinois 1960

Bottomore T B — ELITES AND SOCIETY Watts London 1964

Bottomore T B — KARL MARX Prentice Hall. Englewood Cliffs 1973

Briggs A — 'The language of class in early 19th century England' in Briggs A and Saville J ed: ESSAYS IN LABOUR HISTORY Macmillan London 1960

Crosland C A R — THE FUTURE OF SOCIALISM Cape London 1956

Dahrendorf R — CLASS AND CLASS CONFLICT IN INDUSTRIAL SOCIETY Routledge and Kegan Paul London 1959

Frankel H — CAPITALIST SOCIETY AND MODERN SOCIOLOGY Lawrence and Wishart London 1970

Giddens Anthony — THE CLASS STRUCTURE OF ADVANCED SOCIETIES Hutchinson London 1973

Goldthorpe J H — 'Social stratification in industrial society' in Halmos P ed THE DEVELOPMENT OF INDUSTRIAL SOCIETIES Sociological Review Monograph 8 1964

Goldthorpe J H — 'Class, status and party in modern Britain' Archives européennes de sociologie vol XIII 1972 pp 342-372

Goldthorpe J H Lockwood D Bechhofer F and Platt J — THE AFFLUENT WORKER 1968-1969 (3 parts: see under section C 60)

Jackson J A ed — SOCIAL STRATIFICATION (Sociological Studies 1) Cambridge University Press London 1968

Kidron M — WESTERN CAPITALISM SINCE THE WAR Penguin Harmondsworth 1970 (1st ed 1968)

Littlejohn J A — WESTRIGG Routledge and Kegan Paul London 1963

Littlejohn J   SOCIAL STRATIFICATION: AN INTRODUCTION Allen
                               and Unwin London 1972

Lockwood D   THE BLACK-COATED WORKER: A STUDY IN CLASS CONS-
                               CIOUSNESS Allen and Unwin London 1958

Lockwood D   'Sources of variation in working class images
                               of society' Sociological Review 14(3) November
                               1966

Macrae D G   'Social stratification: a trend report and biblio-
                               graphy' Current Sociology 2(1) 1953-54

Marshall T H   CITIZENSHIP AND SOCIAL CLASS Cambridge Univer-
                               sity Press London 1950

Martin D A and Crouch C   'Class and status in modern Britain' in Giner M
                               Scotchford Archer M eds COMPARATIVE EUROPE:
                               CLASS, STATUS AND POWER Weidenfeld and Nicolson
                               London 1970

Marx K   SELECTED WRITINGS IN SOCIOLOGY AND SOCIAL PHILO-
                               SOPHY Bottomore T B and Rubel M eds Penguin
                               Harmondsworth 1956

                               THE 18TH BRUMAIRE OF LOUIS BONAPARTE Interna-
                               tional Publishers New York 1963

Miliband Ralph   THE STATE IN CAPITALIST SOCIETY Weidenfeld
                               and Nicolson London 1969

Ossowski S   CLASS STRUCTURES IN THE SOCIAL CONSCIOUSNESS
                               Routledge and Kegan Paul London 1963

Parkin F   CLASS, INEQUALITY AND POLITICAL ORDER MacGibbon
                               and Kee London 1971 Paladin London 1972

Runciman W G   RELATIVE DEPRIVATION AND SOCIAL JUSTICE: A
                               STUDY OF ATTITUDES TO SOCIAL INEQUALITY IN
                               20TH CENTURY ENGLAND Routledge and Kegan Paul
                               London 1966

Salaman Graeme   'Occupational communities: convenience of work
                               and non-work' Sociological review vol 19 no 3
                               August 1971

Stacey M   TRADITION AND CHANGE: A STUDY OF BANBURY
                               Oxford University Press London 1960

Strachey E J   CONTEMPORARY CAPITALISM Gollancz London 1956

Tawney R H   EQUALITY 4th ed Allen and Unwin London 1964
                               (1st ed 1931)

Turner R H   'Life-situation and subculture: a comparison of merited prestige judgments by three occupational classes in Britain' British Journal of Sociology 9(4) December 1958 (see also Young M and Willmott P 'Social grading by manual workers' British Journal of Sociology December 1965)

Weber M   'Class, status, party' e g in Gerth H H and Mills C W eds FROM MAX WEBER Routledge and Kegan Paul London 1948 and in Bendix R and Lipset S M op cit

Wedderburn Dorothy   POVERTY INEQUALITY AND CLASS STRUCTURE Cambridge University Press London 1974

Westergaard J H   'Some aspects of the study of modern British society' in Rex J ed APPROACHES TO SOCIOLOGY Routledge and Kegan Paul London 1974

Westergaard J H   'The myth of classlessness' in Blackburn R ed IDEOLOGY IN SOCIAL SCIENCE Fontana London 1972

Westergaard J H and Resler Henrietta   CLASS IN CONTEMPORARY BRITAIN Heinemann London 1974

Williams R   THE LONG REVOLUTION Chatto and Windus London 1961

Young M   THE RISE OF THE MERITOCRACY 1870-2033 Penguin Harmondsworth 1961 (1st ed 1958)

C 20   Capital, income and expenditure

C 20   Property and capital
(see also B 32 Mid-19th century income and wealth C 34 Business and private economic power)

Atkinson A B   UNEQUAL SHARES: WEALTH IN BRITAIN Allen Lane London 1972

Campion H   PUBLIC AND PRIVATE PROPERTY IN GREAT BRITAIN Oxford University Press London 1939

Fijalkowski-Bereday G Z   'The equalising effects of the death duties' Oxford Economic Papers 2(2) June 1950

Glyn Andrew and Sutcliffe Bob   BRITISH CAPITALISM, WORKERS AND THE PROFITS SQUEEZE Penguin Harmondsworth 1972

Harbury C D   'Inheritance and the distribution of personal wealth in Britain' Economic Journal 72 (288) December 1962

Klein L R et al   'Savings and finances of the upper income classes' Bulletin of the Oxford University Institute of Statistics 18(4) November 1956

Lydall H F   BRITISH INCOMES AND SAVINGS Blackwell Oxford 1955

Lydall H F and Tipping D G   WEALTH, INCOME AND INEQUALITY Penguin Harmonds-
eds   worth 1973

Meade J E   EFFICIENCY, EQUALITY AND THE OWNERSHIP OF
PROPERTY Allen and Unwin London 1964

Morgan E V   THE STRUCTURE OF PROPERTY OWNERSHIP IN GREAT
BRITAIN Oxford University Press London 1960

Moyle J   THE PATTERN OF ORDINARY SHARE OWNERSHIP 1957-
1960 Cambridge University Press London 1971

Pollard S and Crossley D W   THE WEALTH OF ENGLAND 1085-1966 Batsford
London 1968

Sandford C T   TAXING PERSONAL WEALTH Allen and Unwin London
1971

Townsend Peter and   LABOUR AND INEQUALITY   Fabian Society London
Bosanquet Nicholas eds   1972

Wedgwood J   THE ECONOMICS OF INHERITANCE London School of
Economics London 1939 (1st ed 1929)

C 21 Income

Atkinson A B   THE TAX CREDIT SCHEME AND THE REDISTRIBUTION
OF INCOME Institute for Fiscal Studies
Publication no 9 London 1973

Barna T   THE REDISTRIBUTION OF INCOMES THROUGH PUBLIC
FINANCE IN 1937 Clarendon Press Oxford 1945

Beckerman W ed   LABOUR'S ECONOMIC RECORD 1964-70 Duckworth
London 1972

Bowley A L   WAGES AND INCOME IN THE UNITED KINGDOM SINCE
1860 Cambridge University Press London 1937

Cartter A M   THE REDISTRIBUTION OF INCOME IN POST-WAR BRITAIN:
A STUDY OF THE EFFECTS OF THE CENTRAL GOVERNMENT
FISCAL PROGRAM IN 1948-49 Yale University Press
New Haven 1955

Field Frank ed   LOW PAY Arow London 1973

Jackson Dudley et al   DO TRADE UNIONS CAUSE INFLATION? Cambridge
University Press London 1972

Lydall H F   'The long-term trend in the size distribution
of incomes' Journal of the Royal Statistical
Society series A 122(1) 1959

Lydall H F   'The life cycle in income, saving and asset ownership' Econometrica 23(2) April 1955

Lydall H F   THE STRUCTURE OF EARNINGS Oxford University Press London 1968

Lydall H F and Lansing J B   'A comparison of the distribution of personal income and wealth in the United States and Great Britain' American Economic Review 49(1) March 1959

Nicholson J L   REDISTRIBUTION OF INCOME IN THE UNITED KINGDOM IN 1959, 1957 AND 1953 Bowes and Bowes Cambridge 1965

Nicholson R J   'Distribution of personal income' Lloyds Bank Review January 1967

Phelps-Brown E H and Browne M H   A CENTURY OF PAY: THE COURSE OF PAY AND PRODUCTION IN FRANCE, GERMANY, SWEDEN, THE UNITED KINGDOM AND THE UNITED STATES OF AMERICA 1860-1960 Macmillan London 1969

Pollard S and Crossley C W THE WEALTH OF BRITAIN 1085-1966 Batsford London 1968

Prest A R and Stark T   'Some aspects of income distribution in the United Kingdom since World War II' Manchester School September 1967

Reid G L and ROBERTSON D J FRINGE BENEFITS, LABOUR COSTS AND SOCIAL SECURITY Allen and Unwin London 1965

Routh G   OCCUPATION AND PAY IN GREAT BRITAIN 1906-60 Cambridge University Press London 1965

Seers D   THE LEVELLING OF INCOMES SINCE 1938 Blackwell Oxford 1951

Titmuss R M   INCOME DISTRIBUTION AND SOCIAL CHANGE Allen and Unwin London 1962

Townsend Peter and Bosanquet Nicholas   LABOUR AND INEQUALITY Fabian Society London 1972

United Kingdom: Department of Employment   NEW EARNINGS SURVEYS Annually since 1968 Reports at intervals in Department of Employ-Gazette

United Kingdom: National Board for Prices and Incomes   TOP SALARIES IN THE PRIVATE SECTOR AND NATIONALISED INDUSTRIES (report no 107) HMSO London 1969

United Kingdom   REPORT OF THE COMMITTEE OF INQUIRY INTO THE IMPACT OF RATES ON HOUSEHOLDS HMSO London 1965

United Kingdom: Royal Commission on the Taxation of Profits and Incomes — FINAL REPORT (cmnd 9474 B P P 1955/6 XXVII) HMSO London 1955

United Kingdom — PROPOSALS FOR A TAX CREDIT SCHEME (cmnd 5116) HMSO London 1972

Wootton B — THE SOCIAL FOUNDATIONS OF WAGE POLICY Allen and Unwin London 1955

C 22 Social security and poverty
(see also G Social policy)

Abel-Smith B and Townsend P — THE POOR AND THE POOREST Bell London 1965

Abel-Smith B et al — SOCIALISM AND AFFLUENCE: FOUR FABIAN ESSAYS Fabian Society London 1967

Atkinson A B — POVERTY IN BRITAIN AND THE REFORM OF SOCIAL SECURITY Cambridge University Press London 1970

Bowley A L and Burnett-Hurst A R — LIVELIHOOD AND POVERTY London School of Economics London 1915

Booth C ed — LIFE AND LABOUR OF THE PEOPLE IN LONDON 1892-1903: 1st SERIES — POVERTY (4 vols and map vol) Macmillan London 1902-3

Bull David ed — FAMILY POVERTY Gerald Duckworth London 1972

Coates Ken and Silburn Richard — POVERTY : THE FORGOTTEN ENGLISHMAN Penguin Harmondsworth 1970

Cole D and Utting J — THE ECONOMIC CIRCUMSTANCES OF OLD PEOPLE Codicote Press Welwyn 1962

Kincaid J C — POVERTY AND EQUALITY IN BRITAIN Penguin Harmondsworth 1973

Marsden D — MOTHERS ALONE: POVERTY AND THE FATHERLESS FAMILY Allen and Unwin London 1969

Rowntree B S — POVERTY: A STUDY OF TOWN LIFE 1st ed 1901 2nd ed 1902 new ed Longmans London 1922

Rowntree B S — POVERTY AND PROGRESS: A SECOND SOCIAL SURVEY OF YORK Longmans London 1946 (1st ed 1941)

Rowntree B S and Lavers G R — POVERTY AND THE WELFARE STATE Longmans London 1951

Smith H L ed — THE NEW SURVEY OF LONDON LIFE AND LABOUR 1930-1935 vols 3 and 6 SURVEY OF SOCIAL CONDITIONS London School of Economics London 1932 1934

Titmuss R M — 'The social division of welfare' and 'Pension systems and population change' in idem ESSAYS ON THE WELFARE STATE Allen and Unwin London 1958

Townsend P ed — THE CONCEPT OF POVERTY Heinemann London 1970

United Kingdom — STRATEGY FOR PENSIONS (cmnd 4755) HMSO London 1971

United Kingdom — Annual official analyses of the incidence of taxes and social benefits, published since the 1960's in Economic Trends

Webb Adrian L and Sieve Jack E B — INCOME REDISTRIBUTION AND THE WELFARE STATE Bell London 1971

Wedderburn D — 'Poverty in Britain today: the evidence' Sociological Review 10(3) 1962

Young Michael ed — POVERTY REPORT 1974 Maurice Temple Smith London 1974

Zweig F — LABOUR, LIFE AND POVERTY Gollancz London 1949

C 23 Expenditure and consumption

Crawford W and Broadley H — THE PEOPLE'S FOOD Heinemann London 1938

Drummond J C and Wilbraham A — THE ENGLISHMAN'S FOOD 1938 revised ed Cape London 1958

Ehrenberg A S C and Pyatt F G — CONSUMER BEHAVIOUR Penguin Harmondsworth 1971

Lambert R — NUTRITION IN BRITAIN 1950-60 Codicote Press Welwyn 1964

Orr J Boyd — FOOD, HEALTH AND INCOME Macmillan London 1936

Rock P E — MAKING PEOPLE PAY Routledge and Kegan Paul London 1973

Rowett Research Institute — FAMILY DIET AND HEALTH IN PRE-WAR BRITAIN Carnegie United Kingdom Trust Dunfermline 1955

Soutar M S Wilkins E H and Florence P S — NUTRITION AND THE SIZE OF THE FAMILY Allen and Unwin London 1942

United Kingdom: Ministry of Agriculture, Food and Fisheries — National Food Survey Committee: ANNUAL REPORTS: DOMESTIC FOOD CONSUMPTION AND EXPENDITURE

United Kingdom: Ministry of Labour, now Dept of Employment — FAMILY EXPENDITURE SURVEY now published annually

Young M — 'The distribution of income within the family' British Journal of Sociology 3(4) December 1949

C 30 Power and elites

C 30 General
(see also L 20 The mass media: General)

Anderson P	'Origins of the present crisis' in idem and Blackburn R eds TOWARDS SOCIALISM Collins London 1965 (see also idem 'Components of the national culture' in Cockburn A and Blackburn R eds STUDENT POWER Penguin Harmondsworth 1969)
Annan N	'The intellectual aristocracy' in Plumb J H ed STUDIES IN SOCIAL HISTORY Longmans London 1955
Birnbaum N	'Monarchs and sociologists' Sociological Review vol 3 no 1 July 1955
Bottomore T B	ELITES AND SOCIETY Watts London 1964
Burrage M	'Culture and British economic growth' British Journal of Sociology 20(2) June 1969
Coleman D C	'Gentlemen and players' Economics History Review 26(1) 1973
Dibelius W	ENGLAND Jonathan Cape London 1934
Giddens Anthony	'Elites in the British Class Structure' Sociological Review 2(3) August 1972
Hyman H H	'England and America: climates of tolerance and intolerance' in Bell D ed THE RADICAL RIGHT Doubleday New York 1964
Lerner Daniel and Morton Gordon	EURATLANTICA: CHANGING PERSPECTIVES OF THE EUROPEAN ELITES MIT Press Cambridge Mass 1969
Lipset S M	'The value patterns of democracy' American Sociological Review August 1963 (see also idem THE FIRST NEW NATION Heinemann London 1964)
Martin K	THE CROWN AND THE ESTABLISHMENT Hutchinson London 1962 Penguin Harmondsworth 1963
Perrott R	THE ARISTOCRATS Weidenfeld and Nicolson London 1968
Rothman S	'Modernity and tradition in Britain' Social Research 28(3) Autumn 1961
Sampson A	THE ANATOMY OF BRITAIN Hodder and Stoughton London 1965 (2nd ed)

Shils E   THE TORMENT OF SECRECY Heinemann London 1956

Shils E and Young M   'The meaning of the Coronation' Sociological
                                 Review 1 1953 pp 63-68

Stanworth P and Giddens A   ELITES AND POWER IN BRITISH SOCIETY Cambridge
eds   University Press London 1974

Thomas H ed   THE ESTABLISHMENT New English Library London
                                 1962 (1st ed 1959)

Urry John and Wakeford John   POWER IN BRITAIN Heinemann London 1973

C 31 Political power and elites
(see also F 11 Cabinet and Parliament)

Barnett Anthony   'Class struggle and the Heath Government' New
                                 Left Review 77 Jan/Feb 1973

Crewe Ivor ed   BRITISH POLITICAL SOCIOLOGY YEAR BOOK VOL 1
                                 ELITES IN WESTERN DEMOCRACY Croom Helm London
                                 1973

Guttsman W L   THE BRITISH POLITICAL ELITE MacGibbon and Kee
                                 London 1963

Guttsman W L ed   THE ENGLISH RULING CLASS Weidenfeld and
                                 Nicolson London 1969

Harrison M   TRADE UNIONS AND THE LABOUR PARTY SINCE 1945
                                 Allen and Unwin London 1960

Johnson R W   'The British political elite 1955-1972'
                                 Archives européennes de sociologie XIV no 1
                                 1973

Laski H J   THE BRITISH CABINET: A STUDY OF ITS PERSONNEL
                                 1801-1924 Fabian Society Tract 223 London 1928

McKenzie R T   BRITISH POLITICAL PARTIES Heinemann London
                                 1955 (see also British Journal of Sociology
                                 6(2) June 1955)

Miliband Ralph   PARLIAMENTARY SOCIALISM Allen and Unwin London
                                 1961

Miliband Ralph   THE STATE IN CAPITALIST SOCIETY Weidenfeld
                                 and Nicolson London 1969

Rose Richard   'The making of Cabinet Ministers' British
                                 Journal of Political Science vol 1 part 4
                                 October 1971 pp 393-414

Ross J F S   PARLIAMENTARY REPRESENTATION Eyre and Spottis-
                                 woode London 1943

Ross J F S   ELECTIONS AND ELECTORS Eyre and Spottiswoode
                                 London 1955 (chapters 23-27)

Thomas J A — THE HOUSE OF COMMONS 1832-1901: A STUDY OF ITS ECONOMIC AND FUNCTIONAL CHARACTER Cardiff University Press Cardiff 1939

Wilson C S and Lupton T — 'The social background and connections of "top decision makers"' Manchester School 27(1) January 1959

C 32   The State: Civil Service, Judiciary, the Forces and the Law
(see also K 11 Legal processes, F 12 Civil Service)

Abel Smith B and Stevens R — LAWYERS AND THE COURTS Heinemann London 1967

Abrams P — 'Democracy technology and the retired British officer' in Huntington S P ed CHANGING PATTERNS OF MILITARY POLITICS Free Press of Glencoe New York 1962

Barnett Correlli — BRITAIN AND HER ARMY 1509-1970 Allen Lane London 1970

Blom-Cooper C and Drewry G — FINAL APPEAL Clarendon Press Oxford 1972

Cain Maureen E — SOCIETY AND THE POLICEMAN'S ROLE Routledge and Kegan Paul London 1973

Cohen E N W — THE GROWTH OF THE BRITISH CIVIL SERVICE 1780-1939 Allen and Unwin London 1941

Critchley T A — A HISTORY OF POLICE IN ENGLAND AND WALES Constable London 1967

Judge Anthony — A MAN APART: THE BRITISH POLICEMAN AND HIS JOB Arthur Barker London 1972

Kelsall R K — HIGHER CIVIL SERVANTS IN BRITAIN, FROM 1870 TO THE PRESENT DAY Routledge and Kegan Paul London 1955

Kingsley J D — REPRESENTATIVE BUREAUCRACY Antioch Press Yellow Springs Ohio 1944

McGregor O R et al — SEPARATED SPOUSES: A STUDY OF THE MATRIMONIAL JURISDICTION OF MAGISTRATES' COURTS Duckworth London 1970

Nightingale Benedict — CHARITIES Allen Lane London 1973

Omond J S — PARLIAMENT AND ARMY 1642-1904 Cambridge University Press London 1933

Otley C B — 'Militarism and the social affiliations of the British Army elite' in Van Doorn J ed ARMED FORCES AND SOCIETY: SOCIOLOGICAL ESSAYS Mouton & Co The Hague 1968

Otley C B   'The Social origins of British Army officers'
                        Sociological Review 18(2) July 1970

Otley C B   'The educational background of British Army
                        officers' Sociology 7(2) May 1973

Playfair Giles   SIX STUDIES IN HYPOCRISY Secker and Warburg
                        London 1969

Putnam Robert D   'The political attitudes of senior civil ser-
                        vants in Western Europe; a preliminary report'
                        British Journal of Political Science 3(1973)
                        257-290

Razzell P E   'Social origins of officers in the Indian and
                        British Home Army: 1758-1962' British Journal
                        of Sociology 14(3) September 1963

United Kingdom: Committee   THE CIVIL SERVICE see especially vol 1 Report
on the Civil Service   of the Committee 1966-68 (cmnd 3638) 1968;
(Fulton Committee)   vol 3(1) SOCIAL SURVEY OF THE CIVIL SERVICE
                        by Halsey A H and Crewe I M 1969;
                        vol 3(2) SURVEYS AND INVESTIGATIONS (continued)
                        1968 HMSO London

United Kingdom: Committee   THE METHOD II SYSTEM OF SELECTION FOR THE AD-
of inquiry into Method II   MINISTRATIVE CLASS OF THE HOME CIVIL SERVICE:
selection   REPORT OF THE COMMITTEE OF INQUIRY (cmnd 4156)
                        HMSO London 1969

United Kingdom: House of   6TH REPORT FROM THE ESTIMATES COMMITTEE:
Commons   RECRUITMENT TO THE CIVIL SERVICE HMSO London
                        1965

Watt D C   PERSONALITIES AND POLICIES: STUDIES IN THE
                        FORMULATION OF BRITISH FOREIGN POLICY IN THE
                        TWENTIETH CENTURY Longmans London 1965

C 33   The State: economic control and nationalised industries

Acton Society Trust   STUDIES IN NATIONALISED INDUSTRY: 1-12
                        (see inter alia no 4 MEN ON THE BOARDS)
                        Acton Society Trust London 1950-1953

Britten Samuel   STEERING THE ECONOMY Penguin Harmondsworth 1971

Burrage Michael   'Nationalisation and the professional ideal'
                        Sociology 7(2) May 1973

Friedmann A W and   GOVERNMENT ENTERPRISE: A COMPARATIVE STUDY
Garner J F eds   Stevens London 1970

Hanson A H   NATIONALISATION: A BOOK OF READINGS Allen and Unwin London 1963

Hanson A H   PARLIAMENT AND PUBLIC OWNERSHIP Cassell London 1961

Harris Nigel   COMPETITION AND THE CORPORATE SOCIETY: BRITISH CONSERVATIVES, THE STATE AND INDUSTRY 1945-1964 Methuen London 1972

Jenkins C   POWER AT THE TOP McGibbon and Kee London 1959

Pryke Richard   PUBLIC ENTERPRISE IN PRACTICE MacGibbon and Kee London 1971

Robson William A   NATIONALISED INDUSTRY AND PUBLIC OWNERSHIP Allen and Unwin London 1963

Rogow A A   THE LABOUR GOVERNMENT AND BRITISH INDUSTRY 1945-50 Blackwell Oxford 1955

Shanks M ed   THE LESSONS OF PUBLIC ENTERPRISE Cape London 1963

Smith J H and Chester T E   'The distribution of power in nationalised industries' British Journal of Sociology 2(4) December 1951

Thornhill W   THE NATIONALISED INDUSTRIES: AN INTRODUCTION Nelson London 1968

Tivey Leonard ed   THE NATIONALISED INDUSTRIES SINCE 1960: A BOOK OF READINGS Allen and Unwin London 1973

United Kingdom   FINANCIAL AND ECONOMIC OBLIGATIONS OF THE NATIONALISED INDUSTRIES (cmnd 1337) HMSO London 1961

United Kingdom   NATIONALISED INDUSTRIES, A REVIEW OF ECONOMIC AND FINANCIAL OBJECTIVES (comnd 3437) HMSO London 1967

United Kingdom: Select Committee on Nationalised Industries   FIRST REPORT SESSION 1967-1968 MINISTERIAL CONTROL OF NATIONALISED INDUSTRIES vol 1 Report and proceedings of the Committee HMSO London
(and subsequent reports)

31

C 34 Business and private economic power
(see also D 20 Industrial organisation and management and D 21 Internal
organisation and management)

Aaronovitch S   MONOPOLY Lawrence and Wishart London 1965

Aaronovitch S   THE RULING CLASS Lawrence and Wishart London
                           1961

Acton Society Trust   MANAGEMENT SUCCESSION Acton Society Trust 1956

Barratt Brown M   'The limits of the welfare state'; 'The con-
                           trollers of British industry' in Coates K ed
                           CAN THE WORKERS RUN INDUSTRY Sphere London
                           1969

Blackburn Robin   'The new capitalism' in Blackburn Robin ed
                           IDEOLOGY IN SOCIAL SCIENCE Fontana London 1972

Brady R A   BUSINESS AS A SYSTEM OF POWER Columbia Univer-
                           sity Press New York 1943

Clements R V   MANAGERS: A STUDY OF THEIR CAREERS IN INDUSTRY
                           Allen and Unwin London 1958

Copeman G H   LEADERS OF BRITISH INDUSTRY Geo and Co London
                           1955

Crosland C A R   THE FUTURE OF SOCIALISM Jonathan Cape London
                           1958

Erickson C J   BRITISH INDUSTRIALISTS: STEEL AND HOSIERY 1850-
                           1950 Cambridge University Press London 1959

Finer S E   'The political power of private capital'
                           Sociological Review 3(2) 4(1) December 1955
                           July 1956

Florence P Sargant   OWNERSHIP CONTROL AND SUCCESS OF LARGE COMPANIES
                           Sweet and Maxwell London 1961

Galbraith J K   THE NEW INDUSTRIAL STATE Hamish Hamilton London
                           1967

Hodges Michael   MULTINATIONAL CORPORATIONS AND NATIONAL GOVERN-
                           MENTS: A CASE STUDY OF THE UNITED KINGDOM'S
                           EXPERIENCE 1964-1970 Saxon House Farnborough 1974

Nichols T   OWNERSHIP CONTROL AND IDEOLOGY Allen Unwin
                           London 1969

Parkinson H   OWNERSHIP OF INDUSTRY Eyre and Spottiswoode
                           London 1951

Schonfield A   MODERN CAPITALISM: THE CHANGING BALANCE OF PUBLIC
                           AND PRIVATE POWER Oxford University Press London
                           1965

Whitley Richard   'Commonalities and connections among Directors
                           of large financial institutions' Sociological
                           Review 21(4) November 1973

C 40   The Professions
(see also E 50 Further and higher education)

Abel-Smith B   A HISTORY OF THE NURSING PROFESSION Heinemann
                                    London 1960

Abel-Smith B and Stevens R LAWYERS AND THE COURTS Heinemann London 1967

Abel-Smith B and Stevens R IN SEARCH OF JUSTICE Allen Lane London 1968

Baron G and Tropp A   'Teachers in England and America' in Halsey A H
                            et al eds EDUCATION, ECONOMY AND SOCIETY Free
                            Press New York 1965

Ben-David J   'Professions in the class system of present-
                            day societies' Current Sociology 12(3) 1963-64

Bernbaum G   THE HEADMASTERS Publisher and date of publi-
                            cation to be announced

Box S and Cotgrove S   'Scientific identity, occupational selection
                            and role strain' British Journal of Sociology
                            17(1) March 1966

Brown C K F   HISTORY OF THE ENGLISH CLERGY 1800-1900 Faith
                            Press London 1953

Carr-Saunders A M and   THE PROFESSIONS Clarendon Press Oxford 1933
Wilson P A

Coats A W and Coats S E   'The social composition of the Royal Economic
                            Society and the beginnings of the British
                            Economics profession 1890-1915' British
                            Journal of Sociology March 1970

Coats A W and Coats S E   'The changing social composition of the Royal
                            Economic Society 1890-1960 and the professionali-
                            sation of British Economics' British Journal
                            of Sociology June 1973

Coates R D   TEACHERS' UNIONS AND INTEREST GROUP POLITICS
                            Cambridge University Press London 1972

Elias N   'Studies in the genesis of the naval profession'
                            British Journal of Sociology 1(4) December 1950

Elliott Philip   THE SOCIOLOGY OF THE PROFESSIONS Macmillan
                            London 1972

Floud J and Scott W   'Recruitment to teaching in England and Wales'
                            in Halsey A H et al eds EDUCATION, ECONOMY AND
                            SOCIETY Free Press New York 1965

Gerstl J E and Hutton S P   ENGINEERS: THE ANATOMY OF A PROFESSION Tavistock
                            Publications London 1966

Halsey A H and Trow M   THE BRITISH ACADEMICS Faber London 1971

Hastings A and Hinnings C R   'Role relations and value adaptation: a study
                               of the professional accountant in industry'
                               Sociology 4(3) September 1970

Hickson D J and Thomas   'Professionalisation in Britain: a preliminary
M W   measure' Sociology 3(1) January 1969

Jackson J A ed   PROFESSIONS AND PROFESSIONALISM Cambridge Uni-
                               versity Press London 1970

Johnson Terence J   PROFESSIONS AND POWER Macmillan London 1972

Kelsall R K   'Self-recruitment in four professions' in
                               Glass D V ed SOCIAL MOBILITY IN BRITAIN
                               Routledge and Kegan Paul London 1954

King M D   'Science and the professional dilemma' in
                               Gould S J ed PENGUIN SOCIAL SCIENCES SURVEY
                               1968 Penguin Harmondsworth 1968

Lewis R and Maude A   PROFESSIONAL PEOPLE Phoenix House London 1952

Lipman Alan   'Architecural education and the social com-
                               mitments of contemporary British Architecture'
                               Sociological Review vol 18 no 1 March 1970

Little E M   HISTORY OF THE BRITISH MEDICAL ASSOCIATION 1832-
                               1932 British Medical Association London 1933

Manzer Ronald A   TEACHERS AND POLITICS Manchester University
                               Press Manchester 1970

Marshall T H   'The recent history of professionalism' in idem
                               CITIZENSHIP AND SOCIAL CLASS Cambridge Univer-
                               sity Press London 1950

Millerson G   THE QUALIFYING ASSOCIATIONS Routledge and Kegan
                               Paul London 1964

Musgrove Frank and Taylor   SOCIETY AND THE TEACHERS ROLE Routledge and
Philip H   Kegan Paul London 1969

Pavey A E   THE STORY OF THE GROWTH OF NURSING Faber London
                               1953

Prandy K   PROFESSIONAL EMPLOYEES: A STUDY OF SCIENTISTS
                               AND ENGINEERS Faber London 1965

Scott W   'Fertility and social mobility among teachers'
                               Population Studies 11(13) 1958

Tropp A   THE SCHOOLTEACHERS Heinemann London 1957
                               (see also YEAR-BOOK OF EDUCATION Evans Bros
                               London 1953)

Tunstall Jeremy

JOURNALISTS AT WORK Constable London 1971

United Kingdom: Royal Commission on Doctors' and Dentists' Remuneration 1957-1960

REPORT (cmnd 939) HMSO London 1960 (especially Appendices)

Werskey Paul Gary

'British Scientists and "outsider" politics 1931-1945' in Barnes Barry ed SOCIOLOGY OF SCIENCE Penguin Harmondsworth 1972

Wicksteed J H

THE GROWTH OF A PROFESSION: THE CHARTERED SOCIETY OF PHYSIOTHERAPY 1894-1945 Edward Arnold London 1948

Wilensky H

'The professionalisation of everyone' American Journal of Sociology September 1964

Zander M

LAWYERS AND THE PUBLIC INTEREST Weidenfeld and Nicolson London 1968

C 50   The Middle classes

Bechhofer F and Elliott B

'An approach to a study of small shopkeepers and the class structure' European Journal of Sociology 9(2) 1968

Blackburn R M

UNION CHARACTER AND SOCIAL CLASS: A STUDY OF WHITE COLLAR UNIONISM Batsford London 1967

Bonham J

THE MIDDLE CLASS VOTE Faber London 1954

Bonham J and Martin F M

'Two studies in the middle class vote' British Journal of Sociology 3(3) September 1952

Dale J R

THE CLERK IN INDUSTRY Liverpool University Press Liverpool 1962

Grossmith G W

THE DIARY OF NOBODY Collins London 1955 (1st ed 1895)

Kelsall R K et al

'The new middle class in the power structure of Great Britain' Transactions 3rd World Congress of Sociology vol III 1956

Klingender F D

THE CONDITION OF CLERICAL LABOUR IN BRITAIN Lawrence London 1935

Lewis R and Maude A E

THE ENGLISH MIDDLE CLASSES Phoenix House London 1950 (1st ed 1949)

Lockwood D

THE BLACKCOATED WORKER: A STUDY IN CLASS CONSCIOUSNESS Allen and Unwin London 1958

Masterman C F G   'The suburbanites' in idem THE CONDITION OF ENGLAND Methuen London 1960 (1st ed 1909)

Raynor J   THE MIDDLE CLASS Longmans London 1969

Sykes A J M   'Some differences in the attitudes of clerical and of manual workers' Sociological Review 13 1965 pp 297-310

Woodward J   THE SALESWOMAN Pitman London 1960

C 60   The working class
(see also D 30 Work and the labour market   D 41 History and organisation of Trade Unions   D 42 Industrial disputes)

Anderson P and Blackburn R eds   TOWARDS SOCIALISM Collins London 1965 (see especially Part I chapters by Anderson, Westergaard, Blackburn. See also Miliband R and Saville J eds: THE SOCIALIST REGISTER Merlin Press London 1965 Chapters by Wedderburn and Thompson)

Arnot R P   THE MINERS: A HISTORY OF THE MINERS' FEDERATION OF GREAT BRITAIN 1889-1910 Allen and Unwin London 1949

Arnot R P   THE MINERS: YEARS OF STRUGGLE, 1910 ONWARDS Allen and Unwin London 1953

Arnot R P   THE MINERS: IN CRISIS AND WAR FROM 1930 ONWARDS Allen and Unwin London 1961

Bakke E W   CITIZENS WITHOUT WORK Yale University Press New Haven 1940

Bauman Z   BETWEEN CLASS AND ELITE: THE EVOLUTION OF THE BRITISH LABOUR MOVEMENT Manchester University Press Manchester 1972

Bell Colin and Newby Howard   'The sources of variation in Agricultural Workers' images of Society' Sociological Review 21(2) May 1972

Bell F E E   AT THE WORKS Edward Arnold London 1907 Nelson London 1911

Benney M   CHARITY MAIN: A COALFIELD CHRONICLE Allen and Unwin London 1946

Brennan T et al   SOCIAL CHANGE IN SOUTH WEST WALES Watts London 1954

Briefs G A   THE PROLETARIAT MacGraw Hill New York and London 1937

Briggs A ed	CHARTIST STUDIES Macmillan London 1959
Brown Richard and Bannen Peter	'Social relations and social perspectives amongst shipbuilding workers – a preliminary statement' Part 1 Sociology 4(1) January 1970 Part 2 Sociology 4(2) May 1970
Brown R K Bannen P Cousins J M and Samphier M L	'The contours of solidarity: social stratification and industrial relations in shipbuilding' British Journal of Industrial Relations March 1972
Bulmer Martin ed	STUDIES IN WORKING CLASS IMAGERY Routledge and Kegan Paul London 1974
Cannon I C	'Ideology and occupational community: a study of compositors' Sociology 1(2) May 1967
Cole G D H	A SHORT HISTORY OF THE BRITISH WORKING CLASS MOVEMENT Allen and Unwin London 1948
Dennis N et al	COAL IS OUR LIFE Eyre and Spottiswoode London 1956
Downes D	THE DELINQUENT SOLUTION Routledge and Kegan Paul London 1965
Dufty N F ed	THE SOCIOLOGY OF THE BLUE COLLAR WORKER E J Brill Holland 1969
Engels F	THE CONDITION OF THE WORKING CLASSES IN ENGLAND Oxford University Press London 1971
Goldthorpe J H et al	THE AFFLUENT WORKER: 1 INDUSTRIAL ATTITUDES AND BEHAVIOUR Cambridge University Press London 1968 2 POLITICAL ATTITUDES AND BEHAVIOUR Cambridge University Press London 3 THE AFFLUENT WORKER IN THE CLASS STRUCTURE Cambridge University Press London 1969
Kemeny Paul James	'The affluent worker project: some criticisms and a derivative study' Sociology Review vol 20 no 3 August 1972
Gould Tony and Kenyon Joe	STORIES FROM THE DOLE QUEUE Maurice Temple Smith London 1972
Hill M J with Harrison R M Sargeant A V and Talbot V	MEN OUT OF WORK: A STUDY OF UNEMPLOYMENT IN THREE ENGLISH TOWNS Cambridge University Press London 1973
Hobsbawm E J	'The labour aristocracy in nineteenth century Britain' in Saville J ed DEMOCRACY AND THE LABOUR MOVEMENT Lawrence and Wishart London 1954

Hobsbaw E J	LABOURING MEN Weidenfeld and Nicolson London 1964
Hoggart R	THE USES OF LITERACY Chatto and Windus London 1958
Hollowell P G	THE LORRY DRIVER Routledge and Kegan Paul London 1968
Ineichen Bernard	'Home ownership and manual workers' life-styles' Sociological Review 20(3) August 1972
Jackson B	WORKING CLASS COMMUNITY Routledge and Kegan Paul London 1968
Jeffreys J B	THE STORY OF ENGINEERS 1800-1945 Lawrence and Wishart London 1945
Jones Mervyn	LIFE ON THE DOLE Davis-Poynter London 1972
Kerr M	THE PEOPLE OF SHIP STREET Routledge and Kegan Paul London 1968
Klein J	SAMPLES FROM ENGLISH CULTURES Routledge and Kegan Paul London 1965
Lambert R S and Beales H L eds	MEMOIRS OF THE UNEMPLOYED Gollancz London 1934
Liverpool University: Social Science Dept	THE DOCK WORKER Liverpool University Press Liverpool 1954
Lockwood D	'Sources of variation in working class images of society' Sociological Review 14(3) November 1966
Mann Michael	CONSCIOUSNESS AND ACTION AMONG THE WESTERN WORKING CLASS Macmillan London 1973
Moorhouse Bert Wilson Mary and Chamberlain Chris	'Rent strikes — direct action and the working class' Miliband Ralph and Saville John eds SOCIALIST REGISTER 1972 Merlin Press London 1972
Nairn Tom	'The English working class' in Blackburn Robin ed IDEOLOGY IN SOCIAL SCIENCE Fontana London 1972
Newby Howard	'Agricultural workers in the class structure' Sociological Review 20(3) August 1972
Orwell G	THE ROAD TO WIGAN PIER Penguin Harmondsworth 1962 (1st ed 1937)
Reeves M S Pember	ROUND ABOUT A POUND A WEEK Bell London 1913

Rice M Spring	WORKING CLASS WIVES Penguin Harmondsworth 1939
Rose G	THE WORKING CLASS Longmans London 1969
Runciman W G	RELATIVE DEPRIVATION AND SOCIAL JUSTICE Routledge and Kegan Paul London 1966
Sykes A J M	'Navvies: work attitudes and social relations' Sociology 3(1-2) January-May 1969
Thompson E P	THE MAKING OF THE ENGLISH WORKING CLASS Gollancz London 1963 (revised Pelican edition 1968)
Tunstall J	THE FISHERMEN McGibbon and Kee London 1962
Westergaard J H	'The rediscovery of the cash nexus' in Miliband R and Saville J eds THE SOCIALIST REGISTER 1970 Merlin Press London 1970
Zweig F	THE BRITISH WORKER Penguin Harmondsworth 1952
Zweig F	THE WORKER IN AN AFFLUENT SOCIETY Heinemann London 1961

C 70   Social Mobility

(see also C 30 - 34 Power and elites   C 40 The professions   E 60 Educational selection and social mobility   E 70   Entry to employment)

Abbot J	'The concept of mobility' Sociological Review 14(2) 1966
Ashby A W and Jones J M	'The social origins of farmers in Wales' Sociological Review 18(2) April 1926
Benjamin B	'Inter-generation differences in occupation' Population Studies 11(3) March 1958
Berent J	'Fertility and social mobility' Population Studies 5(3) March 1952
Chapman S J and Marquis F J	'The recruiting of the employing classes from the ranks of the wage earner in the cotton industry' Journal of the Royal Statistical Society 75(3) February 1912
Glass D V ed	SOCIAL MOBILITY IN BRITAIN Routledge and Kegan Paul London 1954
Gibson John	'Biological aspects of a high socio-economic group' Journal of Biosocial science 2(1) January 1970
Gibson John B and Mascie-Taylor C G Nicholas	'Biological aspects of a high socio-economic group II - IQ components and social mobility' Journal of Biosocial Science 5(1) January 1973

Ginsberg M   'Interchange between social classes' in idem
                                    STUDIES IN SOCIOLOGY Methuen London 1932

Lipset S M and Bendix R   SOCIAL MOBILITY IN INDUSTRIAL SOCIETY Heinemann
                                    London 1960

Lockwood D   'Social mobility' in Welford A T et al ed
                                    SOCIETY Routledge and Kegan Paul London 1962

Miller S M   'Comparative social mobility' Current Socio-
                                    logy 9(1) 1960

Noble Trevor   'Social mobility and class relations in Britain'
                                    British Journal of Sociology December 1972

Oxford Studies in Social   THE ANALYSIS OF SOCIAL MOBILITY: METHODS AND
Mobility: Hope Keith ed   APPROACHES Oxford Studies in Social Mobility,
                                    Working Papers vol I Oxford University Press
                                    London 1972

Oxford Studies in Social   MOBILITY IN BRITAIN RECONSIDERED Oxford Studies
Mobility: Ridge J M ed   in Social Mobility, Working Papers Vol II
                                    Oxford University Press London 1974

Thomas D   'The social origins of marriage partners of
                                    the British peerage in 18th and 19th centuries'
                                    Population Studies 26(1) March 1972

D ECONOMIC AND INDUSTRIAL ORGANISATION

D 10 General

Burns T ed	INDUSTRIAL MAN Penguin Harmondsworth 1969
Burns T	'On the plurality of social systems' in Lawrence J R ed OPERATIONAL RESEARCH AND THE SOCIAL SCIENCES Tavistock Publications London 1966
Burns T	'The sociology of industry' in Welford A T et al eds SOCIETY Routledge and Kegan Paul London 1962
Child J	THE BUSINESS ENTERPRISE IN MODERN INDUSTRIAL SOCIETY Collier Macmillan London 1970
Florence P S	ECONOMICS AND SOCIOLOGY OF INDUSTRY Watts London 1964
Lipton M	ASSESSING ECONOMIC PERFORMANCE Staples Press London 1968
Musgrave P W	THE ECONOMIC STRUCTURE Longmans London 1970
Parker S R Brown R K Child J and Smith M A	THE SOCIOLOGY OF INDUSTRY Allen and Unwin London 1967 (revised ed 1973)

D 20 The structure of industry and economic control
(see also C 20 Property and capital C 33 and C 34)

Allen G C	MONOPOLY AND RESTRICTIVE PRACTICES Allen and Unwin London 1968
Allen G C	THE STRUCTURE OF INDUSTRY IN BRITAIN Longmans London 1966 (2nd ed)
Armstrong A and Silbertson A	'Size of plant, size of enterprise and concentration in British manufacturing industry 1935-58' Journal of the Royal Statistical Society Series A 128(3) 1965
Blackburn Robin	'The new capitalism' in Blackburn Robin ed IDEOLOGY IN SOCIAL SCIENCE Fontana London 1972
Burn D	THE STRUCTURE OF BRITISH INDUSTRY London 1960
Carter C F and Williams B R	INDUSTRY AND TECHNICAL PROGRESS Oxford University Press London 1958
Dunning J H and Thomas G J	BRITISH INDUSTRY Hutchinson London 1961 (2nd ed 1963)

Evely R W and Little I M D   CONCENTRATION IN BRITISH INDUSTRY Cambridge
University Press London 1960

Florence P S   LOGIC OF BRITISH AND AMERICAN INDUSTRY Routledge and Kegan Paul London 1961

George K D   'Changes in British industrial concentration
1951-1958' Journal of Industrial Economics
15(3) July 1967

Jervis F R   THE ECONOMICS OF MERGERS Routledge and Kegan
Paul London 1971

Jones Robert and Marriott
Oliver   ANATOMY OF A MERGER: A HISTORY OF G E C, A E I
AND ENGLISH ELECTRIC Jonathan Cape London 1970

Leak H and Maizels A   'The structure of British industry' Journal
of the Royal Statistical Society 108(1-2) 1945

Political and Economic
Planning (PEP)   GOVERNMENT AND INDUSTRY PEP London 1952

Smith R Brooks D and
Stewart R G   MERGERS (Acton Society Trust series):
no 1   PAST AND PRESENT 1963
no 2   THE HUMAN EFFECTS OF MERGERS: THE IMPACT
ON MANAGERS 1963
no 3   THE HUMAN EFFECTS OF MERGERS: THE IMPACT
ON THE SHOP FLOOR 1966
All published by Acton Society Trust London

Teeling-Smith G ed (Office
of Health Economics)   SCIENCE, INDUSTRY AND THE STATE Pergamon Oxford
1965

United Kingdom: Board of
Trade   CENSUSES OF PRODUCTION: REPORTS   HMSO London

D 21   Internal organisation and management

Acton Society Trust   MANAGEMENT INITIATIVE Acton Society Trust London 1961

Acton Society Trust   MANAGEMENT SUCCESSION Acton Society Trust London 1956

Acton Society Trust   MANAGEMENT UNDER NATIONALISATION Acton Society
Trust London 1953

Bendix R   WORK AND AUTHORITY IN INDUSTRY Chapman and Hall
London 1956

Brown W D B   EXPLORATIONS IN MANAGEMENT Heinemann London
1961

Burns T and Stalker G M   THE MANAGEMENT OF INNOVATION Tavistock Publications London 1961

Burrage M

'Culture and British economic growth' British Journal of Sociology 20(2) June 1969

Child J

BRITISH MANAGEMENT THOUGHT: A CRITICAL ANALYSIS Allen and Unwin London 1969 (see also Sociological Review 16(2) July 1968)

Clark D G

THE INDUSTRIAL MANAGER – HIS BACKGROUND AND CAREER PATTERN Business Publications London 1966 ('Some inter-industry comparisons...' British Journal of Industrial Relations July 1968)

Clements R V

MANAGERS Allen and Unwin London 1958

Cotgrove Stephen and Box Steven

SCIENCE INDUSTRY AND SOCIETY: STUDIES IN THE SOCIOLOGY OF SCIENCE Allen and Unwin London 1970

Ingham G K

SIZE OF INDUSTRIAL ORGANISATION AND WORKER BE- HAVIOUR Cambridge University Press London 1970

Kelly J

IS SCIENTIFIC MANAGEMENT POSSIBLE? Faber Lon- don 1968

McGivering I C et al

MANAGEMENT IN BRITAIN Liverpool University Press Liverpool 1960

Milward G E ed

LARGE SCALE ORGANISATION Macdonald and Evans London 1950

National Institute of Industrial Psychology

THE FOREMAN: A STUDY OF SUPERVISION IN BRITISH INDUSTRY Staples Press London 1951

Scott W H

MANAGEMENT IN BRITAIN: A CHARACTERISATION Liver- pool University Press Liverpool 1960

Shenfield Barbara

COMPANY BOARDS: THEIR RESPONSIBILITIES TO SHARE- HOLDERS EMPLOYEES AND THE COMMUNITY Allen and Unwin London 1971

Smith J H

'Sociology and management studies' British Jour- nal of Sociology June 1960

Sofer Cyril

MEN IN MID-CAREER Cambridge University Press London 1970

Urwick L and Brech E F L

THE MAKING OF SCIENTIFIC MANAGEMENT 3 vols Management Publications Trust London 1945-1948

Woodward Joan

MANAGEMENT AND TECHNOLOGY HMSO London 1958

Woodward Joan

INDUSTRIAL ORGANISATION: THEORY AND PRACTICE Oxford University Press London 1965

Woodward Joan

INDUSTRIAL ORGANISATION: BEHAVIOUR AND CONTROL Oxford University Press London 1970

43

D 30 Work and the labour market
(see also C 40 Professions C 50 The middle classes C 60 The working
class E 60 Educational selection and social mobility E 70 Entry to
employment H 70 Position and employment of women)

Banks O — THE ATTITUDE OF STEELWORKERS TO TECHNICAL CHANGE Liverpool University Press Liverpool 1960

Benyon Huw — WORKING FOR FORD Allen Lane London 1973

Blackburn R M and Benyon H — PERCEPTIONS OF WORK VARIATIONS WITHIN A FACTORY Cambridge University Press London 1972

Cunnison S — WAGES AND WORK ALLOCATION Tavistock Publications London 1966

Fox Alan — A SOCIOLOGY OF WORK IN INDUSTRY Collier-Macmillan London 1971

Handyside J D and Speak M — 'Job satisfaction: myths and realities' British Journal of Industrial Relations 2(1) March 1964

Harris A I and Clausen R — LABOUR MOBILITY IN GREAT BRITAIN Government Social Survey HMSO London 1966

Jefferys M — MOBILITY IN THE LABOUR MARKET Routledge and Kegan Paul London 1954

Kahn H — REPERCUSSIONS OF REDUNDANCY Allen and Unwin London 1964

Lupton T — ON THE SHOP FLOOR Pergamon Oxford 1963

Mann Michael — WORKERS ON THE MOVE: THE SOCIOLOGY OF RELOCATION Cambridge University Press London 1973

Martin Roderick and Fryer R H — REDUNDANCY AND PATERNALIST CAPITALISM Allen and Unwin London 1973

Mumford E and Banks O — THE COMPUTER AND THE CLERK Routledge and Kegan Paul London 1967

Parker Stanley — THE FUTURE OF WORK AND LEISURE MacGibbon and Kee London 1971

Rhee H A — OFFICE AUTOMATION IN SOCIAL PERSPECTIVE Blackwell Oxford 1968

Roberts B C and Smith J H eds — MANPOWER POLICY AND EMPLOYMENT TRENDS Bell London 1966

Rose J — AUTOMATION: ITS USES AND CONSEQUENCES Oliver and Boyd Edinburgh 1967

Sadler P	SOCIAL RESEARCH ON AUTOMATION Heinemann London 1968
Scott W H et al	TECHNICAL CHANGE AND INDUSTRIAL RELATIONS Liverpool University Press Liverpool 1956
Stieber J ed	EMPLOYMENT PROBLEMS OF AUTOMATION AND ADVANCED TECHNOLOGY Macmillan London 1966
United Kingdom: Social Survey (Reports, new series) Thomas G	No 134: LABOUR MOBILITY IN GREAT BRITAIN, 1945-1949 2 parts HMSO London 1952
Walker N	MORALE IN THE CIVIL SERVICE Edinburgh University Press Edinburgh 1961
Warner Malcolm ed	THE SOCIOLOGY OF THE WORKPLACE Allen and Unwin London 1973
Wedderburn Dorothy	REDUNDANCY AND THE RAILWAYMEN Cambridge University Press London 1965
Wedderburn Dorothy	WHITE-COLLAR REDUNDANCY Cambridge University Press London 1964
Wedderburn Dorothy and Crompton Rosemary	WORKERS' ATTITUDES AND TECHNOLOGY Cambridge University Press London 1972
Weir David ed	MEN AND WORK IN MODERN BRITAIN Fontana London 1974

D 40   Industrial relations

D 40   General

Acton Society Trust	THE FRAMEWORK OF JOINT CONSULTATION Acton Society Trust London 1952
Allen V L	THE SOCIOLOGY OF INDUSTRIAL RELATIONS Longman London 1971
Alexander K J W and Jenkins C L	FAIRFIELDS: A STUDY OF INDUSTRIAL CHANGE Allen Lane London 1970
Balfour Campbell	UNIONS AND THE LAW Saxon House Farnborough 1973
Banks J A	MARXIST SOCIOLOGY IN ACTION: A SOCIOLOGICAL CRITIQUE OF THE MARXIST APPROACH TO INDUSTRIAL RELATIONS Faber and Faber London 1970
Blain A N J	PILOTS AND MANAGEMENT: INDUSTRIAL RELATIONS IN THE U K AIRLINES Allen and Unwin London 1972

Clegg H — THE SYSTEM OF INDUSTRIAL RELATIONS IN BRITAIN Blackwell Oxford 1970

Cliff Tony — THE EMPLOYERS' OFFENSIVE: PRODUCTIVITY DEALS AND HOW TO FIGHT THEM Pluto Press London 1970

Cotgrove Stephen Dunham Jack and Vamplew Clive — THE NYLON SPINNERS: A CASE STUDY ON PRODUCTIVITY BARGAINING AND JOB ENLARGEMENT Allen and Unwin London 1971

Flanders Allan — MANAGEMENT AND UNIONS: THE THEORY AND REFORM OF INDUSTRIAL RELATIONS Faber London 1970

Flanders Allan — THE FAWLEY PRODUCTIVITY AGREEMENTS Faber London 1964

Flanders Allan and Clegg H — THE SYSTEM OF INDUSTRIAL RELATIONS IN GREAT BRITAIN Blackwell Oxford 1954 (e g chapter by Kahn-Freund; see also idem in Ginsberg M ed LAW AND OPINION IN THE TWENTIETH CENTURY Stevens and Sons London 1959)

Hill George Hobday Peter and Hamway John — INDUSTRIAL RELATIONS: THE BOARDROOM VIEWPOINT Bodley Head London 1972

Roberts B C — INDUSTRIAL RELATIONS Methuen London 1966

Scase Richard — 'Industrial man: a reassessment with English and Swedish data' British Journal of Sociology June 1972

Scott W H — INDUSTRIAL LEADERSHIP AND JOINT CONSULTATION Liverpool University Press Liverpool 1952

Turner H A et al — LABOUR RELATIONS IN THE MOTOR INDUSTRY Allen and Unwin London 1967

United Kingdom: Royal Commission on trade unions and employers' associations 1965-1968 (Donovan Commission) — REPORT (Cmnd 3623) 1968 RESEARCH PAPERS (see especially no 1 McCarthy W E J THE ROLE OF SHOP STEWARDS... 1966; no 3 Fox A INDUSTRIAL SOCIOLOGY AND INDUSTRIAL RELATIONS 1966; no 6 Bain G S TRADE UNION GROWTH AND RECOGNITION WITH SPECIAL REFERENCE TO WHITE-COLLAR UNIONS IN PRIVATE INDUSTRY 1967; no 10 McCarthy W E J and Parker S R SHOP STEWARDS AND WORKSHOP RELATIONS 1968)
(See also WRITTEN EVIDENCE OF THE MINISTRY OF LABOUR 1965)
All HMSO London

United Kingdom: Secretary of State for Employment and Productivity — IN PLACE OF STRIFE (Cmnd 3888) HMSO London 1969

Wedderburn K W — THE WORKER AND THE LAW Penguin Harmondsworth 1965

D 41 History and organisation of Trade Unions
(see also C 60 The working class and B 42 19th century working class organisations)

Allen V L	MILITANT TRADE UNIONISM Merlin Press London 1966
Allen V L	POWER IN TRADE UNIONS Longmans London 1954
Allen V L	TRADE UNIONS AND THE GOVERNMENT Longmans London 1960
Allen V L	TRADE UNION LEADERSHIP Longmans London 1958
Bain George S Coates David and Ellis Valerie	SOCIAL STRATIFICATION AND TRADE UNIONISM Heinemann Educational Books London 1973
Bain George Sayers	'Union growth and employment trends in the United Kingdom 1964-1970' British Journal of Industrial Relations November 1972
Bain George Sayers	THE GROWTH OF WHITE-COLLAR UNIONISM Oxford University Press London 1970
Banks J A	TRADE UNIONISM Collier-Macmillan London 1973
Blackburn R and Cockburn A eds	THE INCOMPATIBLES: TRADE UNION MILITANCY AND THE CONSENSUS Penguin Harmondsworth 1967
Blackburn R M	UNION CHARACTER AND SOCIAL CLASS: A STUDY OF WHITE COLLAR UNIONISM Batsford London 1967
Bullock A	THE LIFE AND TIMES OF ERNEST BEVIN Heinemann London 1960-1967
Clegg H A	GENERAL UNION Blackwell Oxford 1954
Clegg H A et al	A HISTORY OF BRITISH TRADE UNIONS SINCE 1889 vol I: 1889-1910 Oxford University Press London 1964
Clegg H A Killick A J and Adams R	TRADE UNION OFFICERS Blackwell Oxford 1961
Flanders A	TRADE UNIONS Hutchinson London 1968 (revised ed)
Goldstein J	THE GOVERNMENT OF BRITISH TRADE UNIONS Allen and Unwin London 1952
Goodman J F B and Whittingham T G	SHOP STEWARDS IN BRITISH INDUSTRY McGraw Hill New York 1969
Harrison M	TRADE UNIONS AND THE LABOUR PARTY SINCE 1945 Allen and Unwin London 1960
Hinton James	THE FIRST SHOP STEWARDS MOVEMENT Allen and Unwin London 1973

Hyman Richard	THE WORKERS' UNION 1898-1929 Oxford University Press London 1971
Marsh A	MANAGERS AND SHOP STEWARDS Institute of Personnel Management London 1963
Marsh A and Coker E	'Shop steward organisation in the engineering industry' British Journal of Industrial Relations 1(2) June 1963
Ostergaard G N and Halsey A H	POWER IN COOPERATIVES Blackwell Oxford 1965
Pribicevic B	THE SHOP STEWARDS' MOVEMENT AND WORKERS' CONTROL 1910-1922 Blackwell Oxford 1959
Richter Irving	POLITICAL PURPOSE IN TRADE UNIONS Allen and Unwin London 1973
Roberts B C	TRADE UNION GOVERNMENT AND ADMINISTRATION IN GREAT BRITAIN Bell London 1956
Roberts B C Loveride Ray and Gonnard John	RELUCTANT MILITANTS Heinemann London 1972
Webb S and B	THE HISTORY OF TRADES UNIONISM 1666-1920 4th ed 1950 Longmans London (1st ed 1920)
Wootton G	'Parties in Union Government: the AESD' Political Studies 9(2) 1961

D 42   Industrial disputes

Buchan Alasdair	THE RIGHT TO WORK Calder and Boyers London 1972
Eldridge J E T	INDUSTRIAL DISPUTES Routledge and Kegan Paul London 1968
Farman Christopher	THE GENERAL STRIKE: MAY 1926 Hart-Davis St Albans 1972
Galambos P and Evans E W	'Work stoppages in the United Kingdom 1950-1964' Bulletin of the Oxford Institute of Economics and Statistics 28(1) February 1966 (see also Knowles K C G ibid vol 28 no 2)
Hyman Richard	'Industrial conflict and political economy' in Saville J and Miliband R eds SOCIALIST REGISTER 1973 Merlin Press London 1973
Hyman Richard	STRIKES Fontana/Collins London 1972
Ingham G K	STRIKES AND INDUSTRIAL CONFLICT Macmillan London 1974

Kerr C and Siegel A   'The inter-industry propensity to strike — an
                             international comparison' in Kornhauser A et al
                             eds INDUSTRIAL CONFLICT McGraw Hill New York
                             1954

Knowles K G J C   STRIKES Blackwell Oxford 1952

Lane Tony and Roberts   STRIKE AT PILKINGTONS Fontana London 1971
Kenneth

Lockwood D   'Arbitration and industrial conflict' British
                             Journal of Sociology 6(4) December 1955

Ross A M and Hartmann P T   CHANGING PATTERNS OF INDUSTRIAL CONFLICT Wiley
                             Gordon House London 1960

Scott W H et al   COAL AND CONFLICT Liverpool University Press
                             Liverpool 1963

Silver Michael   'Recent British strike trends: a factual ana-
                             lysis' British Journal of Industrial Relations
                             March 1973

Turner H A   IS BRITAIN REALLY STRIKE PRONE? University of
                             Cambridge Department of Applied Economics
                             Occasional Papers no 20 Cambridge 1969

D 43 Workers 'participation'

Banks J A   INDUSTRIAL PARTICIPATION: A CASE STUDY Liver-
                             pool University Press Liverpool 1963

Blumberg Paul   INDUSTRIAL DEMOCRACY: THE SOCIOLOGY OF PARTI-
                             CIPATION Constable London 1968

Clarke R O Fatchett D J   WORKERS PARTICIPATION IN MANAGEMENT IN BRITAIN
and Roberts B C   Heinemann London 1972

Clegg H A   INDUSTRIAL DEMOCRACY AND NATIONALISATION Black-
                             well Oxford 1951

Clegg H A   A NEW APPROACH TO INDUSTRIAL DEMOCRACY Blackwell
                             Oxford 1960

Coates K ed   CAN THE WORKERS RUN INDUSTRY? Sphere London 1969

Flanders A et al   EXPERIEMENT IN INDUSTRIAL DEMOCRACY Faber London
                             1968

E EDUCATION
(see also B 40 Social institutions in the mid 19th century: education and schools)

E 10 General

Adamson J W   ENGLISH EDUCATION 1789-1902 Cambridge University
                                     Press London 1930

Banks O   THE SOCIOLOGY OF EDUCATION Batsford London 1968

Barker Rodney   EDUCATION AND POLITICS 1900-1951: A STUDY OF
                                     THE LABOUR PARTY Oxford University Press Lon-
                                     don 1972

Baron G   SOCIETIES, SCHOOLS AND PROGRESS IN ENGLAND
                                     Pergamon Oxford 1965

Bell Robert, Fowler Gerald   EDUCATION IN GREAT BRITAIN AND IRELAND Rout-
and Little Ken eds   ledge and Kegan Paul London 1973

Blaug M   AN INTRODUCTION TO THE ECONOMICS OF EDUCATION
                                     Allen Lane London 1970

Broadheart G D   'Social class factors in special education'
                                     Journal of Biosocial science 4(3) July 1972

Cowan Douglas Duddihy Bob   THE RED PAPER Islander Publications Edinburgh
Lindsay Colin eds   1970

Cox C B and Dyson A E eds   BLACK PAPERS ON EDUCATION Davis-Poynter Lon-
                                     don 1971

Curtis S J   HISTORY OF EDUCATION IN GREAT BRITAIN Uni-
                                     versity Tutorial Press London 1948

Curtis S J   EDUCATION IN BRITAIN SINCE 1900 Dakers London
                                     1952

Floud J and Halsey A H   'The sociology of education: a trend report
                                     and bibliography' Current Sociology 7(3)
                                     1958

Glass D V   'Education and social change in modern England'
                                     in Ginsberg M LAW AND OPINION IN ENGLAND IN
                                     THE 20TH CENTURY Stevens London 1959 (also in
                                     Halsey A H et al ed below)

Halsey A H et al ed   EDUCATION, ECONOMY AND SOCIETY Free Press New
                                     York 1965

Halsey A H ed   EDUCATIONAL PRIORITY Department of Education
                                     and Science HMSO London 1972

Hans N   COMPARATIVE EDUCATION Routledge and Kegan
                                     Paul London 1949

Hopper E I ed — READINGS IN THE THEORY OF EDUCATIONAL SYSTEMS Hutchinson London 1971

Kelsall R K and H M — THE SCHOOL TEACHER IN ENGLAND AND THE UNITED STATES: THE FINDINGS OF EMPIRICAL RESEARCH Pergamon Press Oxford 1969

King R A — EDUCATION Longmans London 1970

Lawson John and Silver Harold — A SOCIAL HISTORY OF EDUCATION IN ENGLAND Methuen London 1973

Murphy James — CHURCH STATE AND SCHOOLS IN BRITAIN 1800-1970 Routledge and Kegan Paul London 1971

Musgrave P W — SOCIETY AND EDUCATION IN ENGLAND AND WALES SINCE 1800 Methuen London 1968

Musgrave P W — SOCIOLOGY HISTORY AND EDUCATION: A READER Methuen London 1970

Musgrove Frank — PATTERNS OF POWER AND AUTHORITY IN ENGLISH EDUCATION Methuen London 1971

Osborne G S — SCOTTISH AND ENGLISH SCHOOLS: A COMPARATIVE SURVEY OF THE PAST FIFTY YEARS Longmans London 1966

Peacock A et al — EDUCATIONAL FINANCE: ITS SOURCES AND USES IN THE UNITED KINGDOM Oliver and Boyd Edinburgh 1968

Raynor John and Harden Jane — READINGS IN URBAN EDUCATION vol 1 City communities and the young vol 2 Equality and city schools Routledge and Kegan Paul/Oxford University Press London 1973

Silver Harold — THE CONCEPT OF POPULAR EDUCATION MacGibbon and Kee London 1965

Silver Pamela and Harold — THE EDUCATION OF THE POOR: THE HISTORY OF A NATIONAL SCHOOL 1824-1974 Routledge and Kegan Paul London 1974

Simon B — EDUCATION AND THE LABOUR MOVEMENT 1870-1920 Lawrence and Wishart London 1965

Simon B — STUDIES IN THE HISTORY OF EDUCATION 1780-1870 Lawrence and Wishart London 1960

Simon Joan — THE SOCIAL ORIGINS OF ENGLISH EDUCATION Routledge and Kegan Paul London 1970

United Kingdom: Department of Education and Science — STATISTICS OF EDUCATION annually

Vaizey J — THE COSTS OF EDUCATION Allen and Unwin London 1958

Wardle David — ENGLISH POPULAR EDUCATION 1780-1970 Cambridge University Press London 1970

Wardle David — THE RISE OF THE SCHOOLED SOCIETY Routledge and Kegan Paul London 1974

Young M ed — KNOWLEDGE AND CONTROL Collier-Macmillan London 1971

E 20 Nursery, elementary and primary education

Blackstone Tessa — A FAIR START: THE PROVISION OF PRE-SCHOOL EDUCATION Allen Lane, Penguin Press London 1971

Blyth W A L — ENGLISH PRIMARY EDUCATION Routledge and Kegan Paul London 1965

Lowndes G A N — THE SILENT SOCIAL REVOLUTION Oxford University Press London 1937

Selleck R J W — ENGLISH PRIMARY EDUCATION AND THE PROGRESSIVES 1914-1939 Routledge and Kegan Paul London 1972

Sturt M — THE EDUCATION OF THE PEOPLE Routledge and Kegan Paul London 1967

Tropp A — THE SCHOOL TEACHERS Heinemann London 1956

United Kingdom: Department of Education and Science, Central Advisory Council for Education (England) — CHILDREN AND THEIR PRIMARY SCHOOLS: 1 REPORT 2 RESEARCH AND SURVEYS (Plowden Report) HMSO London 1967

E 30 Secondary education

Archer R L — SECONDARY EDUCATION IN THE NINETEENTH CENTURY Cambridge University Press London 1921

Armitage P — RAISING THE SCHOOL LEAVING AGE, COMPREHENSIVE REORGANISATION AND THE DEMAND FOR HIGHER EDUCATION London School of Economics London 1971

Banks O — PARITY AND PRESTIGE IN THE ENGLISH SECONDARY EDUCATION Routledge and Kegan Paul London 1955

Batley R, O'Brien O and Parris A — GOING COMPREHENSIVE Routledge and Kegan Paul London 1970

Benn Caroline and Simon Brian   HALF WAY THERE: REPORT ON THE BRITISH COMPREHENSIVE SCHOOL REFORM Penguin Harmondsworth 1972 (2nd ed)

Berg L   RISINGHILL: DEATH OF A COMPREHENSIVE SCHOOL Penguin Harmondsworth 1968

Campbell F   ELEVEN PLUS AND ALL THAT Watts London 1956

Ford J   SOCIAL CLASS AND THE COMPREHENSIVE SCHOOL Routledge and Kegan Paul London 1969

Davis R   THE GRAMMAR SCHOOL Penguin Harmondsworth 1967

Hargreaves D H   SOCIAL RELATIONS IN A SECONDARY SCHOOL Routledge and Kegan Paul London 1967

Holly D N   'Profiting from a comprehensive school' British Journal of Sociology 16(2) June 1965 see also 16(4) December 1965

Holly D N   SOCIETY, SCHOOLS AND HUMANITY: THE CHANGING WORLD OF SECONDARY EDUCATION MacGibbon and Kee London 1971

James E now Lord   EDUCATION AND LEADERSHIP Harrap London 1951

King Ronald   VALUES AND INVOLVEMENT IN A GRAMMAR SCHOOL Routledge and Kegan Paul London 1969

King Ronald   SCHOOL ORGANISATION AND PUPIL INVOLVEMENT: A STUDY OF SECONDARY SCHOOLS Routledge and Kegan Paul London 1973

Lacey C   HIGHTOWN GRAMMAR: THE SCHOOL AS A SOCIAL SYSTEM Manchester University Press Manchester 1970

Monks T G   COMPREHENSIVE EDUCATION IN ENGLAND AND WALES: A SURVEY OF SCHOOLS AND THEIR ORGANISATION National Foundation of Educational Research in England and Wales Slough 1968

Pedley R   THE COMPREHENSIVE SCHOOL Penguin Harmondsworth 1963

Rubinstein David and Simon Brian   THE EVOLUTION OF THE COMPREHENSIVE SCHOOL Routledge and Kegan Paul London 1969

Simon Brian   INTELLIGENCE TESTING AND THE COMPREHENSIVE SCHOOL Lawrence and Wishart London 1953

Stevens Frances   THE LIVING TRADITION Hutchinson London 1960

Stevens Frances   THE NEW INHERITORS Hutchinson London 1970

Taylor W   THE SECONDARY MODERN SCHOOL Faber London 1963

United Kingdom: Ministry   15 TO 18 (Crowther Report) 2 vols HMSO London
of Education Central   1959-60
Advisory Council

United Kingdom: Ministry   HALF OUR FUTURE (Newsom Report) HMSO London
of Education Central Ad-   1963
visory Council (England)

E 40   The Independent schools

Bamford T W   THE RISE OF THE PUBLIC SCHOOLS Nelson London
1967
(see also idem British Journal of Sociology
12(3) September 1961)

Bishop T J H and   WINCHESTER AND THE PUBLIC SCHOOL ELITE Faber
Wilkinson R   London 1967

Glennester H and Wilson G   PAYING FOR PRIVATE SCHOOLS Allen Lane London
1970

Kalton G   THE PUBLIC SCHOOLS: A FACTUAL SURVEY Longmans
London 1966

Kamm Josephine   INDICATIVE PAST: A HUNDRED YEARS OF THE GIRLS'
PUBLIC DAY SCHOOL TRUST Allen and Unwin London
1972

Lambert R   THE STATE AND BOARDING EDUCATION Methuen London 1966

Lambert R et al   NEW WINE IN OLD BOTTLES? STUDIES IN INTEGRATION
WITHIN THE PUBLIC SCHOOLS (Occasional Papers
on Social Administration no 28) Bell London
1968

Mack E C   PUBLIC SCHOOLS AND BRITISH OPINION vol I:
1780-1860 Methuen London 1938, vol II: since
1860 Columbia University Press New York 1941

United Kingdom: Board   THE PUBLIC SCHOOLS AND THE GENERAL EDUCATIONAL
of Education, Committee   SYSTEM (Fleming Report) HMSO London 1944
on Public Schools

United Kingdom: Public   FIRST REPORT: vol I REPORT   vol II APPENDICES
Schools Commission   HMSO London 1968
      SECOND REPORT HMSO London 1970

| Wakeford J | THE CLOISTERED ELITE: A SOCIOLOGICAL ANALYSIS OF THE ENGLISH PUBLIC BOARDING SCHOOL Macmillan London 1969 |

| Weinberg I | THE ENGLISH PUBLIC SCHOOLS: THE SOCIOLOGY OF ELITE EDUCATION Atherton Press New York 1967 |

| Wilkinson R | THE PREFECTS Oxford University Press London 1964 |

E 50   Further and Higher Education: organisation and policy

| Argles M | SOUTH KENSINGTON TO ROBBINS:... TECHNICAL AND SCIENTIFIC EDUCATION SINCE 1851 Longmans London 1964 |

| Armytage W H G | CIVIC UNIVERSITIES Ernest Benn London 1955 |

| Ashby E | TECHNOLOGY AND THE ACADEMICS Macmillan London 1960 |

| Barnard G A and McCreath Margaret D | 'Subject commitments and the demand for higher education' Journal of the Royal Statistical Society Series A (general) vol 133 part 3 1970 |

| Barnes Barry ed | THE SOCIOLOGY OF SCIENCE Penguin Harmondsworth 1972 |

| Burgess Tyrell and Pratt John | POLICY AND PRACTICE: THE COLLEGES OF ADVANCED TECHNOLOGY Allen Lane London/Penguin Harmondsworth 1970 |

| Butcher H J and Rudd Ernest eds | CONTEMPORARY PROBLEMS IN HIGHER EDUCATION: AN ACCOUNT OF RESEARCH McGraw-Hill New York 1972 |

| Cardwell D S L | THE ORGANISATION OF SCIENCE IN ENGLAND Heinemann London 1957 (revised 1972) |

| Collison P and Millen J | 'University Chancellors: a social people' Sociology 3(1) 1969 |

| Cotgrove S | TECHNICAL EDUCATION AND SOCIAL CHANGE Allen and Unwin London 1958 |

| European Journal of Sociology | Special issue on universities 3(1) 1962 |

| Green V H H | THE UNIVERSITIES Penguin Harmondsworth 1969 |

| Halsey A H and Trow M | THE BRITISH ACADEMICS Faber London 1971 |

| Harrison J F C | LEARNING AND LIVING 1790-1960: A STUDY IN THE HISTORY OF THE ENGLISH ADULT EDUCATION MOVEMENT Routledge and Kegan Paul London 1961 |

Harrison M J and Weightman Keith   'Academic freedom and higher education in England' British Journal of Sociology 25(1) March 1974

Kneller G F   HIGHER LEARNING IN BRITAIN Cambridge University Press London 1955

Layard R et al   THE IMPACT OF ROBBINS: EXPANSION IN HIGHER EDUCATION Penguin Harmondsworth 1969

Lomax D E ed   THE EDUCATION OF TEACHERS IN BRITAIN Wiley Chichester 1973

Lynch James and Plunkett H Dudley   TEACHER EDUCATION AND CULTURAL CHANGE Allen and Unwin London 1973

Marris P   THE EXPERIENCE OF HIGHER EDUCATION Routledge and Kegan Paul London 1964

Martin D A ed   ANARCHY AND CULTURE: THE PROBLEM OF THE CONTEMPORARY UNIVERSITY Routledge and Kegan Paul London 1969

Moberly W   THE CRISIS IN THE UNIVERSITY SCM Press London 1949

Moodie Graeme C and Eustace Rowland   POWER AND AUTHORITY IN BRITISH UNIVERSITIES Allen and Unwin London 1974

Moore W G   THE TUTORIAL SYSTEM AND ITS FUTURE Pergamon Oxford 1968

Oxford University   COMMISSION OF INQUIRY: REPORT (Franks Report) Oxford University Press London 1966

Oxford University   REPORT OF THE COMMITTEE ON RELATIONS WITH JUNIOR MEMBERS (Hart Committee) Oxford University Press London 1969

Pratt John and Burgess Tyrrell   POLYTECHNICS Pitman London 1974

Robbins L Lord   THE UNIVERSITY IN THE MODERN WORLD Macmillan London 1966

Robinson E   THE NEW POLYTECHNICS - THE PEOPLE'S UNIVERSITIES Cornmarket Press London 1968

Rose Hilary and Rose Steven   SCIENCE AND SOCIETY Allen Lane London 1969

Rothblatt S   THE REVOLUTION OF THE DONS: CAMBRIDGE AND SOCIETY IN VICTORIAN ENGLAND Faber London 1968

Sanderson Michael — THE UNIVERSITIES AND BRITISH INDUSTRY 1850-1970 Routledge and Kegan Paul London 1972

Sociological Review — Monograph 7: SOCIOLOGICAL STUDIES IN BRITISH UNIVERSITY EDUCATION October 1963 (see e g Newfield)

Taylor William — SOCIETY AND THE EDUCATION OF TEACHERS Faber and Faber London 1969

Thompson E P — WARWICK UNIVERSITY LTD: INDUSTRY, MANAGEMENT, AND CONTROL Penguin Harmondsworth 1970

Tillyard A I — A HISTORY OF UNIVERSITY REFORM FROM 1800 TO THE PRESENT TIME Heffer and Jones Cambridge 1913

Truscot B — REDBRICK UNIVERSITY Penguin Harmondsworth 1951

Tunstall Jeremy ed — THE OPEN UNIVERSITY OPENS Routledge and Kegan Paul London 1974

United Kingdom: Committee on Higher Education (Robbins Committee) — HIGHER EDUCATION, REPORT 1963 and APPENDICES 1963-4 e g Appendix I THE DEMANDS...; II STUDENTS... (cmnd 2154 and 2154 I to IV) HMSO London 1963-64

E 51 Further and Higher Education : Students

Abbott Joan — STUDENT LIFE IN A CLASS SOCIETY Pergamon Oxford 1970

Archer M S ed — STUDENTS, UNIVERSITY AND SOCIETY: A COMPARATIVE SOCIOLOGICAL REVIEW Heinemann London 1972

Ashby Eric and Anderson Mary — THE RISE OF THE STUDENT ESTATE IN BRITAIN Macmillan London 1970

Blackstone Tessa, Gales Kathleen, Hadley Roger and Lewis Wyn — STUDENTS IN CONFLICT: L S E in 1967 Weidenfeld and Nicolson London 1970

Brothers Joan and Hatch Stephen — RESIDENCE AND STUDENT LIFE Tavistock London 1971

Cockburn A and Blackburn R eds — STUDENT POWER: PROBLEMS, DIAGNOSIS, ACTION Penguin Harmondsworth 1969 (see inter alia Anderson P COMPONENTS OF THE NATIONAL CULTURE)

Hajnal J — THE STUDENT TRAP Penguin Harmondsworth 1972

Hoch P and Schoenbach V — L S E, THE NATIVES ARE RESTLESS Sheed and Ward London 1969

Hornsey College of Art (Staff and Students) — THE HORNSEY AFFAIR Penguin Harmondsworth 1969

Kidd H — THE TROUBLE AT L S E 1966-1967 Oxford University Press London 1969

Nagel Julian ed — STUDENT POWER Merlin London 1969

United Kingdom: Select Committee on Education and Science (House of Commons) — STUDENT RELATIONS: VOL I: REPORT HMSO London 1969

Wilson Bryan — THE YOUTH CULTURE AND THE UNIVERSITIES Faber and Faber London 1970

Zweig Ferdynand — THE STUDENT IN SOCIETY Heinemann London 1963

E 60 Educational selection and social mobility
(see also C 70 Social mobility)

Banks Olive and Finlayson Douglas — SUCCESS AND FAILURE IN THE SECONDARY SCHOOL Methuen London 1973

Bernstein Basil — CLASS CODES AND CONTROL Vol I Routledge and Kegan Paul London 1971

Bernstein Basil ed — CLASS CODES AND CONTROL Vol II Routledge and Kegan Paul London 1973

Brandis Walter and Bernstein Basil — SELECTION AND CONTROL Routledge and Kegan Paul London 1974

Brandis Walter and Henderson D — SOCIAL CLASS LANGUAGE AND COMMUNICATION Routledge and Kegan Paul London 1970

Byrne D S and Williamson W — 'Some inter-regional variations in educational Provision and their bearing upon educational attainment – the case of the North East' Sociology 6(1) January 1972

Cook-Gumperz Jenny — SOCIAL CONTROL AND SOCIALISATION: A STUDY OF CLASS DIFFERENCES IN THE LANGUAGE OF MATERNAL CONTROL Routledge and Kegan Paul London 1973

Craft M ed — FAMILY CLASS AND EDUCATION Longman London 1970

Dale R R and Griffith S — DOWN STREAM: FAILURE IN THE GRAMMAR SCHOOL Humanities Press London 1965

Douglas J W B — THE HOME AND THE SCHOOL MacGibbon and Kee London 1964

Douglas J W B et al — ALL OUR FUTURE: A LONGITUDINAL STUDY OF SECONDARY EDUCATION Peter Davies London 1968

Ferri Elsa — STREAMING: TWO YEARS LATER National Foundation for Educational Research Slough 1971

Floud J E and Halsey A H — 'Intelligence tests, social class and selection for secondary schools' British Journal of Sociology 8(1) 1957

Floud J et al — SOCIAL CLASS AND EDUCATIONAL OPPORTUNITY Heinemann London 1956

Furneaux W D — THE CHOSEN FEW: AN EXAMINATION OF SOME ASPECTS OF UNIVERSITY SELECTION IN BRITAIN Oxford University Press London 1961

Glass D V ed — SOCIAL MOBILITY IN BRITAIN Routledge and Kegan Paul London 1954 (chapters V, VI, VII and X)

Halsey A H ed — ABILITY AND EDUCATIONAL OPPORTUNITY (OECD) HMSO London 1961 (e g Chapter 4)

Hogben L ed — POLITICAL ARITHMETIC 1938 (chapters VIII, IX, X)

Hopper E I ed — READINGS IN THE THEORY OF EDUCATIONAL SYSTEMS Hutchinson London 1971

Hordley Irene and Lee D J — 'The "alternative route" — social change and opportunity in technical education' Sociology 4(1) January 1970

Jackson B — STREAMING: AN EDUCATION SYSTEM IN MINIATURE Routledge and Kegan Paul London 1964

Jackson B and Marsden D — EDUCATION AND THE WORKING CLASS Routledge and Kegan Paul London 1962

Kelsall R K — REPORT ON AN ENQUIRY INTO APPLICATIONS FOR ADMISSION TO UNIVERSITIES Association of Universities of the British Commonwealth London 1957

Kelsall R K and Kelsall Helen M — SOCIAL DISADVANTAGE AND EDUCATIONAL OPPORTUNITY Holt Reinhart and Winston London 1971

Lawton D — SOCIAL CLASS LANGUAGE AND EDUCATION Routledge and Kegan Paul London 1968

Leybourne G C and White K — EDUCATION AND THE BIRTH RATE Jonathan Cape London 1940

Lindsay K — SOCIAL PROGRESS AND EDUCATIONAL WASTE London School of Economics London 1926

Lunn J C Barker — STREAMING IN THE PRIMARY SCHOOL National Foundation for Educational Research Slough 1970

MacPherson J S — ELEVEN-YEAR-OLDS GROW UP University of London Press London 1958

Mays J B — EDUCATION AND THE URBAN CHILD Liverpool University Press Liverpool 1962

Musgrove F — THE FAMILY, EDUCATION AND SOCIETY Routledge and Kegan Paul London 1966

Robinson W P and Rackstraw S J — A QUESTION OF ANSWERS 2 vols Routledge and Kegan Paul London 1972

Scottish Council for Research in education, Mental Survey Committee (J Maxwell) — SOCIAL IMPLICATIONS OF THE 1947 SCOTTISH MENTAL SURVEY University of London Press London 1963

EDUCATIONAL AND OTHER ASPECTS OF THE 1947 SCOTTISH MENTAL SURVEY University of London Press London 1958

Silver Harold ed — EQUAL OPPORTUNITY IN EDUCATION Methuen London 1973

United Kingdom: Ministry of Education, Central Advisory Council — EARLY LEAVING HMSO London 1954

Vernon P E ed British Psychological Society — SECONDARY SCHOOL SELECTION Methuen London 1957

Wedge Peter and Prosser Hilary — BORN TO FAIL Arow London 1973

Westergaard J H and Little A N — 'Educational opportunity and social selection in England and Wales: trends and policy implications' in OECD Study Group in the Economics of Education ed SOCIAL OBJECTIVES IN EDUCATIONAL PLANNING HMSO London 1967 (also in British Journal of Sociology 15(4) December 1964 and in Craft M ed FAMILY CLASS AND EDUCATION Longman London 1970 above)

Yates A and Pidgeon D A — ADMISSION TO GRAMMAR SCHOOLS National Council for Educational Research in England and Wales London 1957

E 70   Entry to employment
(see also D 30 Work and the labour market)

Acton Society Trust Collins A et al — THE ARTS GRADUATE IN INDUSTRY Acton Society Trust London 1962

Berg Ivar — EDUCATION AND JOBS: THE GREAT TRAINING ROBBERY Penguin Harmondsworth 1973

Blaug M et al — THE UTILISATION OF EDUCATED MANPOWER IN INDUSTRY Oliver and Boyd Edinburgh 1967

Box S and Ford J — 'Commitment to science: a solution to student marginality?' Sociology 1(3) September 1967

Carter M P	INTO WORK Penguin Harmondsworth 1956
Carter M P	HOME, SCHOOL AND WORK Pergamon Oxford 1962
Collins M	STUDENTS INTO TEACHERS Routledge and Kegan Paul London 1969
Ferguson T and Cunnison J	THE YOUNG WAGE EARNER Oxford University Press London 1951
Ferguson T and Cunnison J	IN THEIR EARLY TWENTIES Oxford University Press London 1956
Kelsall R K Poole Anne and Kuhn Annette	GRADUATES: THE SOCIOLOGY OF AN ELITE Methuen London 1972
Kelsall R K Poole Anne and Kuhn Annette	SIX YEARS AFTER Sheffield University Department of Sociological Studies Sheffield 1970
Lee D J	'Industrial training and social class' Sociological Review 14(3) 1966
Liepmann K	APPRENTICESHIP Routledge and Kegan Paul London 1960
Maizels Joan	ADOLESCENT NEEDS AND THE TRANSITION FROM SCHOOL TO WORK Athlone Press London 1970
Payne G L	BRITAIN'S SCIENTIFIC AND TECHNOLOGICAL MANPOWER Oxford University Press London 1960
Political and Economic Planning (PEP)	GRADUATE EMPLOYMENT: A SAMPLE SURVEY PEP London 1956
	GRADUATES IN INDUSTRY PEP London 1957
Roberts Kenneth	FROM SCHOOL TO WORK: A STUDY OF THE YOUTH EMPLOYMENT SERVICES David and Charles Newton Abbott 1972
United Kingdom: Committee on Manpower Resources for Science and Technology	THE FLOW INTO EMPLOYMENT OF SCIENTISTS, ENGINEERS AND TECHNOLOGISTS (cmnd 3760) HMSO London 1960
United Kingdom: Department of Education and Science: Schools Council	ENQUIRIES 1 : YOUNG SCHOOL LEAVERS HMSO London 1968
Williams G	APPRENTICESHIP IN EUROPE: THE LESSON FOR BRITAIN Chapman and Hall London 1963
Williams G	RECRUITMENT TO SKILLED TRADES Routledge and Kegan Paul London 1957
Williams W M ed	OCCUPATIONAL CHOICE Allen and Unwin London 1974

F GOVERNMENT AND POLITICS

F 10 Constitution and Political Machinery
(see also section C 31 Political power and elites)

F 10 General

Amery L S	THOUGHTS ON THE CONSTITUTION Oxford University Press London 1947
Chester D N and Willson F M G	THE ORGANISATION OF BRITISH CENTRAL GOVERNMENT 1914-1956 Allen and Unwin London 1957
Eckstein H	'The Government of Britain' in Beer S H and Ullam A PATTERNS OF GOVERNMENT Random House New York 1963
Greaves H R G	THE BRITISH CONSTITUTION Allen and Unwin London 1955
Kellas James G	THE SCOTTISH POLITICAL SYSTEM Cambridge University Press London 1973
Laski H J	REFLECTION ON THE CONSTITUTION THE HOUSE OF COMMONS THE CABINET THE CIVIL SERVICE Manchester University Press Manchester 1951
Martin K	THE CROWN AND THE ESTABLISHMENT Hutchinson London 1962 Penguin Harmondsworth 1963
Miliband R	THE STATE AND CAPITALIST SOCIETY Weidenfeld and Nicolson London 1969
Punnett R M	BRITISH GOVERNMENT AND POLITICS Heinemann London 1968 (revised ed 1971)
Smellie K B	A HUNDRED YEARS OF ENGLISH GOVERNMENT Gerald Duckworth London 1950

F 11 Cabinet and Parliament
(see also section C 31)

Bray J	DECISION IN GOVERNMENT Gollancz London 1970
Butt R	THE POWER OF PARLIAMENT Constable London 1967
Campion G F M et al	PARLIAMENT: A SURVEY Allen and Unwin London 1951
Campion G F M et al	BRITISH GOVERNMENT SINCE 1918 Allen and Unwin London 1951
Chester D N and Bowering N	QUESTIONS IN PARLIAMENT Oxford University Press London 1962
Hanson A H	PARLIAMENT AND PUBLIC OWNERSHIP Cassell London 1961
Hanson A H and Wiseman H V	PARLIAMENT AT WORK Stevens London 1962
Laski H J	PARLIAMENTARY GOVERNMENT IN ENGLAND: A COMMENTARY Allen and Unwin London 1945 (revised ed 1959)

Leonard Richard and Valentine Herman	THE BACKBENCHER AND PARLIAMENT Macmillan London 1972
Mackintosh J P	THE BRITISH CABINET Stevens London 1962
Morrison H S	GOVERNMENT AND PARLIAMENT: A SURVEY FROM IN- SIDE Oxford University Press London 1954
Nicolson N	PEOPLE AND PARLIAMENT Weidenfeld and Nicolson London 1958
Punnett R M	FRONT-BENCH OPPOSITION Heinemann London 1973
Richards P G	HONOURABLE MEMBERS, A STUDY OF THE BRITISH BACKBENCHERS Faber London 1959
Robson W A	NATIONALISED INDUSTRY AND PUBLIC OWNERSHIP Allen and Unwin London 1960

F 12 Civil service
(see also section C 32)

Brittan S	STEERING THE ECONOMY Penguin Harmondsworth 1971
Brown R G S	THE ADMINISTRATIVE PROCESS IN BRITAIN Methuen London 1970
Chapman Richard A	THE HIGHER CIVIL SERVICE IN BRITAIN Constable London 1970
Gordon Michael R	'Civil Servants, politicians and parties: shortcomings in the British policy process' Comparative Politics IV 1971 29-58
Heclo Hugh and Wildausky Aaron	THE PRIVATE GOVERNMENT OF PUBLIC MONEY Mac- millan London 1974
Kelsall R K	HIGHER CIVIL SERVANTS IN BRITAIN Routledge and Kegan Paul London 1955
Mackenzie W J M and Grove J W D	CENTRAL ADMINISTRATION IN BRITAIN Longman London 1957
Stacey Frank	THE BRITISH OMBUDSMAN Oxford University Press London 1972
Strauss E	THE RULING SERVANTS: BUREAUCRACY IN RUSSIA FRANCE AND BRITAIN Part I and part II (chap- ter 10) Allen and Unwin London 1961
Thomas H ed	CRISIS IN THE CIVIL SERVICE Blond London 1968
United Kingdom	THE CIVIL SERVICE (Report of the Fulton Committee cmnd 3638) HMSO London 1968

F 13 Local government and local politics

Birch A H — SMALL TOWN POLITICS Oxford University Press London 1959

Boaden Noel — URBAN POLICY-MAKING: INFLUENCES ON COUNTY BOROUGHS IN ENGLAND AND WALES Cambridge University Press London 1971

Boaden Noel — 'Innovation and change in English local Government' _Political Studies_ December 1971 416-429

Bulpitt J G — PARTY POLITICS IN ENGLISH LOCAL GOVERNMENT Longman London 1967

Centre for Urban Studies — STATEMENT OF EVIDENCE TO THE ROYAL COMMISSION ON LOCAL GOVERNMENT IN GREATER LONDON Centre for Urban Studies London 1959

Clements R V — LOCAL NOTABLES AND THE CITY COUNCIL: THE ROLE OF BRISTOL'S BUSINESS AND SOCIAL LEADERS IN THE CITY'S GOVERNMENT Macmillan London 1969

Dearlove John — THE POLITICS OF POLICY IN LOCAL GOVERNMENT Cambridge University Press London 1973

Foley Donald L — GOVERNING THE LONDON REGION: REORGANISATION AND PLANNING IN THE 1960's University of California Press Berkeley 1972

Griffith J A G — CENTRAL DEPARTMENTS AND LOCAL DEPARTMENTS Allen and Unwin London 1966

Hampton William — DEMOCRACY AND COMMUNITY: A STUDY OF POLITICS IN SHEFFIELD Oxford University Press London 1970

Jones G W — BOROUGH POLITICS: A STUDY OF THE WOLVERHAMPTON BOROUGH COUNCIL 1888-1964 Macmillan London 1967

Lee J M — SOCIAL LEADERS AND PUBLIC PERSONS: A STUDY OF COUNTY GOVERNMENT IN CHESHIRE SINCE 1888 Oxford University Press London 1963

London School of Economics, Greater London Group — GREATER LONDON PAPERS London School of Economics London 1961

McIntosh M — 'The report of the Royal Commission on Local Government in Greater London' _British Journal of Sociology_ 12(3) September 1961

Morris D S and Newton K — 'The social composition of a city council: Birmingham 1925-1966' _Social and Economic Administration_ January 1971 29-33

Newton K — 'City politics in Britain and the United States'
Political Studies XVII 1969 208-218

Rhodes Gerald ed — THE NEW GOVERNMENT OF LONDON: THE FIRST FIVE
YEARS Weidenfeld and Nicolson London 1972

Rhodes Gerald — THE GOVERNMENT OF LONDON: THE STRUGGLE FOR RE-
FORM Weidenfeld and Nicolson London 1970

Robson W A — THE GOVERNMENT AND MISGOVERNMENT OF LONDON
George Allen and Unwin 1948 (1st ed 1939)

Sharpe J L — A METROPOLIS VOTES London School of Economics
London 1962

Sharpe J L — 'Elected representatives in local Government'
British Journal of Sociology 13(3) September
1962

Sharpe J L ed — VOTING IN CITIES: THE 1964 BOROUGH ELECTIONS
Macmillan London 1967

Smallwood F — GREATER LONDON: THE POLITICS OF METROPOLITAN
REFORM Bobbs-Merrill Indianapolis 1965

Thornhill W ed — THE GROWTH AND REFORM OF ENGLISH LOCAL GOVERN-
MENT Weidenfeld and Nicolson London 1971

United Kingdom: Royal
Commission on Local
Government in Greater
London — REPORT (cmnd 1164) HMSO London 1960

Wiseman H V — LOCAL GOVERNMENT AT WORK Routledge and Kegan
Paul London 1967

F 20 Political movements, Ideology and Political culture

F 20 General

Almond G A and Verba S — THE CIVIC CULTURE Princeton University Press
Princeton 1963

Barry E Eldon — NATIONALISATION IN BRITISH POLITICS: THE
HISTORICAL BACKGROUND Jonathan Cape London
1965

Bealey F Blondel J and
McCann W P — CONSTITUENCY POLITICS: NEWCASTLE-UNDER-LYME
Faber London 1965

Beer S H — 'Great Britain: from governing elite to or-
ganised parties' in Neumann S ed MODERN
POLITICAL PARTIES University of Chicago Press
Chicago 1956

Carter April — DIRECT ACTION AND LIBERAL DEMOCRACY Routledge and Kegan Paul London 1973

Crick B — IN DEFENCE OF POLITICS Penguin Harmondsworth 1964

Goldsworthy David — COLONIAL ISSUES IN BRITISH POLITICS 1945-1961 Clarendon Press Oxford 1971

Guttsman W — BRITISH POLITICAL ELITE MacGibbon and Kee London 1964

Hart Henry C — 'Parliament and nation building: England and India' in Lowenberg Gerhard ed MODERN PARLIAMENTS: CHANGE OR DECLINE? Aldine-Atherton Chicago 1971

Jessop Bob — TRADITIONAL CONSERVATISM AND BRITISH POLITICAL CULTURE Allen and Unwin London 1974

Jones G — THE POLITICAL STRUCTURE Longmans London 1969

Kavanagh Dennis — 'The deferential English: a comparative critique' Government and Opposition 6 1971 333-360

King Anthony — BRITISH POLITICS: PEOPLE PARTY AND PARLIAMENT Heath Boston 1966

King Anthony — 'Ideas institutions and the policies of Governments: a comparative analysis' parts I and II British Journal of Political Science 3 1973 291-313; part III British Journal of Political Science 3 1973 409-424

Mackenzie W J M — POLITICS AND SOCIAL SCIENCE Penguin Harmondsworth 1969

Pelling H — POPULAR POLITICS AND SOCIETY IN LATE VICTORIAN BRITAIN Macmillan London 1969

Rose R ed — STUDIES IN BRITISH POLITICS Macmillan London 1969 (2nd ed)

Rose R — POLITICS IN ENGLAND: AN INTERPRETATION Little and Brown Boston 1964

Rose R — POLICY MAKING IN BRITAIN Free Press New York 1969

Rose R — POLITICS IN ENGLAND TODAY Faber London 1974

Semmel B — IMPERIALISM AND SOCIAL REFORM Allen and Unwin London 1960

Wallas G — HUMAN NATURE AND POLITICS Constable London 1948 (4th ed)

F 21 Parties, party organisation and party conflict

Bailey S D ed — THE BRITISH PARTY SYSTEM: A SYMPOSIUM Hansard Society London 1952

Beer S H — MODERN BRITISH POLITICS: A STUDY OF PARTIES AND PRESSURE GROUPS Faber London 1965

Beer S H — BRITISH POLITICS IN THE COLLECTIVIST AGE Knopf New York 1965

Berry David — THE SOCIOLOGY OF GRASSROOTS POLITICS Macmillan London 1970

Budge Ian — AGREEMENT AND THE STABILITY OF DEMOCRACY Markham Chicago 1970

Budge Ian Brand J A Margolis Michael and Smith A L M — POLITICAL STRATIFICATION AND DEMOCRACY Macmillan London 1972

Finer S E Berrington H B and Bartholomew D J — BACKBENCH OPINION IN THE HOUSE OF COMMONS 1955-1959 Pergamon Oxford 1961

Jennings Sir Ivor — PARTY POLITICS: vol I   APPEAL TO THE PEOPLE
vol II   THE GROWTH OF THE PARTIES
vol III THE STUFF OF POLITICS
all published Cambridge University Press 1960 1961 1962

Lieber Robert J — BRITISH POLITICS AND EUROPEN UNITY: PARTIES ELITES AND PRESSURE GROUPS University of California Press Berkeley 1970

McKenzie R T — BRITISH POLITICAL PARTIES Heinemann London 1955

McKenzie R T — 'Power in British Political Parties' British Journal of Sociology June 1955

Michels R — POLITICAL PARTIES Free Press New York 1968

Nairn Tom — THE LEFT AGAINST EUROPE Penguin Harmondsworth 1973

Ostergaard G N and Halsey A H — POWER IN COOPERATIVES Blackwell Oxford 1965

Ostrogorski M — DEMOCRACY AND THE ORGANISATION OF POLITICAL PARTIES Macmillan London 1902

Ranney R — PATHWAYS TO PARLIAMENT Macmillan London 1965

Roberts Geoffrey K — POLITICAL PARTIES AND PRESSURE GROUPS IN BRITAIN Weidenfeld and Nicolson London 1970

F 22   Conservatives and the Right Wing

Benewick Robert	THE FASCIST MOVEMENT IN BRITAIN Allen Lane London 1973
Cross C	THE FASCISTS IN BRITAIN Barrie and Rockliff London 1961
Hoffmann J D	THE CONSERVATIVE PARTY IN OPPOSITION 1945-1951 MacGibbon and Kee London 1964
Lindsay T F and Harrington Michael	THE CONSERVATIVE PARTY 1918-1970 Macmillan London 1974
McKenzie R T	'The Conservative Party' Political Quarterly July-September 1961
Nairn Tom	'Enoch Powell: the new Right' New Left Review 61 May/June 1970
Raison T ed	CONFLICT AND CONSERVATISM Conservative Political Centre London 1965
Rose R	'The Bow Group's role in British politics' The Western Political Quarterly December 1961
Schwarz John E and Lambert Geoffrey	'The voting behaviour of British Conservative backbenchers' in Patterson Samuel C and Wahlke John C eds COMPARATIVE LEGISLATIVE BEHAVIOUR: FRONTIERS OF RESEARCH Wiley-Interscience New York 1972
White R J	THE CONSERVATIVE TRADITION Kaye London 1950

F 23   Labour and the Left
(see also C 60 The Working class B 42 Working class organisations and D 41 Trade unions)

Anderson P and Blackburn R eds	TOWARDS SOCIALISM Collins London 1965
Bevan A	IN PLACE OF FEAR Heinemann London 1952
Coates Ken	THE CRISIS OF BRITISH SOCIALISM Spokesman Books Nottingham 1972
Cole G D H	A HISTORY OF SOCIALIST THOUGHT vols 1-5 Macmillan London 1953 1954 1956 1958 1960
Cole M I	THE STORY OF FABIAN SOCIALISM Heinemann London 1961
Cole M	THE STORY OF THE FABIAN SOCIETY London 1962

Cowling Maurice	THE IMPACT OF LABOUR 1920-1924 Cambridge University Press London 1971
Crosland C A R	THE CONSERVATIVE ENEMY Jonathan Cape London 1962
Crosland C A R	THE FUTURE OF SOCIALISM Jonathan Cape London 1956
Crossman R H S ed	NEW FABIAN ESSAYS Turnstile Press London 1952
Foot P	THE POLITICS OF HAROLD WILSON Penguin Harmondsworth 1968
Gregory R	MINERS AND BRITISH POLITICS 1906-1914 Oxford University Press London 1968
Hall P G	LABOUR'S NEW FRONTIERS André Deutsch London 1964
Harris Nigel and Palmer John eds	THE WORLD CRISIS: ESSAYS IN REVOLUTIONARY SOCIALISM Hutchinson London 1971
Harrison M	TRADE UNIONS AND THE LABOUR PARTY SINCE 1945 Allen and Unwin London 1960
Harrison R	BEFORE THE SOCIALISTS Routledge and Kegan Paul London 1965
Hennessey B	'Trade unions and the British Labour Party' American Political Science Review December 1955
Hindess Barry	THE DECLINE OF WORKING CLASS POLITICS MacGibbon and Kee London 1971
Janosik E G	CONSTITUENCY LABOUR PARTIES IN BRITAIN Pall Mall Press London 1968
Kendall W	THE REVOLUTIONARY MOVEMENT IN BRITAIN 1900-1921 Weidenfeld and Nicolson London 1969
Mackenzie N et al	CONVICTION MacGibbon and Kee London 1958
McKenzie R T	Political Quarterly special number on the Labour Party July-September 1960
Miliband R	'Socialism and the myth of the golden past' in Miliband R and Saville J eds SOCIALIST REGISTER 1964 Merlin Press London 1964
Miliband R	PARLIAMENTARY SOCIALISM Allen and Unwin London 1961
Newton K	THE SOCIOLOGY OF BRITISH COMMUNISM Allen Lane London 1969

Thompson P — SOCIALISTS LIBERALS AND LABOUR: THE STRUGGLE FOR LONDON 1885-1914 Routledge and Kegan Paul London 1967

Williams R ed — MAY DAY MANIFESTO Penguin Harmondsworth 1968 (revised ed)

F 24 Liberal and 'centrist' parties

Dangerfield G — THE STRANGE DEATH OF LIBERAL ENGLAND Putnam London 1961/Paladin London 1970

Douglas R — THE HISTORY OF THE LIBERAL PARTY 1895-1970 Sidgwick and Jackson London 1971

Rasmussen J S — THE LIBERAL PARTY Constable London 1965

Taverne Dick — THE FUTURE OF THE LEFT: LINCOLN AND AFTER Jonathan Cape London 1974

F 25 Other

Apter David and Joll James eds — ANARCHISM TODAY Macmillan London 1971

Bailey Ron — THE SQUATTERS Penguin Harmondsworth 1973

Hanham H J — SCOTTISH NATIONALISM Faber and Faber London 1969

Nairn Tom — 'Scotland: anomaly in Europe' New Left Review 83 January-February 1974

Nairn Tom — 'Scotland — the three dreams' New Left Review 49

Rover C — WOMEN'S SUFFRAGE AND PARTY POLITICS IN BRITAIN 1866-1914 Routledge and Kegan Paul London 1967

Thayer G — THE BRITISH POLITICAL FRINGE Blond London 1965

F 30 Voting behaviour

Abrams M and Rose R — MUST LABOUR LOSE? Penguin Harmondsworth 1960

Alford R R — PARTY AND SOCIETY Murray London 1964

Allen A J — THE ENGLISH VOTER English Universities Press London 1964

Barry B — SOCIOLOGISTS ECONOMISTS AND DEMOCRACY Collier-Macmillan London 1970

Benney M et al — HOW PEOPLE VOTE Routledge and Kegan Paul London 1956

Birch A H — 'Citizen participation in England and Wales' International Social Science Journal 12(1) 1960

Birch A H and Campbell P — 'Voting behaviour in a Lancashire constituency' British Journal of Sociology September 1950

Blondel J — VOTERS, PARTIES AND LEADERS Penguin Harmondsworth 1965

Bohem K and Mitchell B R — BRITISH PARLIAMENTARY ELECTION RESULTS 1950-1960 Cambridge University Press London 1966

Bonham J — THE MIDDLE CLASS VOTE Faber London 1954

Blumler J G and McQuail D — TELEVISION IN POLITICS: ITS USES AND INFLUENCE Faber and Faber London 1968

Butler D E — 'Voting behaviour and its study in Britain' British Journal of Sociology June 1955

Butler D E — THE ELECTORAL SYSTEM IN BRITAIN SINCE 1918 Oxford University Press London 1962

Butler D E — THE BRITISH GENERAL ELECTION OF 1955 Macmillan London 1955

Butler D E and Rose R — THE BRITISH GENERAL ELECTION OF 1959 Macmillan London 1960

Butler D E and King A — THE BRITISH GENERAL ELECTION OF 1964 Macmillan London 1965

Butler D E and King A — THE BRITISH GENERAL ELECTION OF 1966 Macmillan London 1966

Butler D E and Freeman J — BRITISH POLITICAL FACTS 1900-1968 Macmillan London 1969

Butler D E and Puito-Duschinsky Michael — THE BRITISH GENERAL ELECTION OF 1970 Macmillan London 1971

Butler D E and Stokes D — POLITICAL CHANGE IN BRITAIN Macmillan London 1969

Campbell P et al — 'Voting behaviour in Droylsden' Manchester School of Economics and Social Studies February 1952

Chamberlain Chris — 'The growth of support for the Labour Party' British Journal of Sociology December 1973

Cook Chris and Ramsden John BY-ELECTIONS IN BRITISH POLITICS Macmillan
eds   London 1973

Craig F W S   BRITISH PARLIAMENTARY ELECTION STATISTICS
                             1918-1968 Political Reference Publications
                             Glasgow 1959

Craig F W S   BRITISH PARLIAMENTARY ELECTION RESULTS 1950-
                             1970 Political Reference Publications Chichester
                             1971

Crewe Ivor   'The politics of "affluent" and "traditional"
                             workers in Britain: an aggregate data analysis'
                             British Journal of Political Science 3 1972
                             29-52

Hodder-Williams Richard   PUBLIC OPINION POLLS AND BRITISH POLITICS
                             Routledge and Kegan Paul London 1970

Kavanagh D   CONSTITUENCY ELECTIONEERING IN BRITAIN Longmans
                             London 1970

Kinnear M   THE BRITISH VOTER: AN ATLAS AND SURVEY SINCE
                             1885 Batsford London 1968

Lipset S   and Rokkan S   'Cleavage structure party systems and voter
                             alignments' in Lipset S M and Rokkan S eds
                             PARTY SYSTEMS AND VOTER ALIGNMENTS Collier
                             Macmillan London 1968

McKenzie R T and Silver A   ANGELS IN MARBLE: WORKING CLASS CONSERVATIVES
                             IN URBAN ENGLAND Heinemann Educational London
                             1968

Martin F M and Bonham J   'Studies in the middle class vote' British
                             Journal of Sociology 3(3) September 1952

Milne F M and Mackenzie   STRAIGHT FIGHT A STUDY IN VOTING BEHAVIOUR
H C   Hansard Society London 1954

Milne F M and Mackenzie   MARGINAL SEAT Hansard Society London 1959
H C

Moorhouse H F   'The political incorporation of the British
                             working class' Sociology 7(3) September 1973

Nordlinger E   THE WORKING CLASS TORIES MacGibbon and Kee
                             London 1967

Parkin F   'Working class conservatives: a theory of poli-
                             tical deviance' British Journal of Sociology
                             18(3) September 1967

Piepe A et al   'The location of the proletarian and deferen-
                             tial worker' Sociology 3(2) May 1969

Plowman D E G | 'Allegiance to political parties' _Political Studies_ October 1955

Rush M | THE SELECTION OF PARLIAMENTARY CANDIDATES Nelson London 1969

Trenaman J and McQuail D | TELEVISION AND THE POLITICAL IMAGE: A STUDY OF THE IMPACT OF TELEVISION ON THE 1959 GENERAL ELECTION Methuen London 1961

Vincent J R | POLLBOOKS: HOW VICTORIANS VOTED Cambridge University Press London 1967

F 31 Political socialization and the politics of young people

Abrams P and Little A N | 'The young voter in British politics; the young activist in British politics' _British Journal of Sociology_ 16(2 and 4) June and December 1965

Abramson P | 'The differential political socialisation of English secondary school students' _Sociology of Education_ 40 1967 pp 246-269

Abramson P and Hennessey T M | 'Beliefs about democracy among British Adolescents' _Political Studies_ XVII 1970 pp 239-242

Dennis Jack Lindberg Leon and McCrone Donald | 'Support for Nation and Government among English children' _British Journal of Political Science_ vol 1 part 1 January 1971 pp 25-48 (see also: comment by Budge Ian _British Journal of Political Science_ vol 1 part 3 pp 389-392)

Stradling Robert and Zurick Elia | 'Political and non-political ideals of English primary and secondary school children' _Sociological Review_ 19(2) May 1971

F 40 Pressure groups

Beer S | 'Pressure groups and parties in Britain' _American Political Science Review_ March 1956

Christoph J B | CAPITAL PUNISHMENT AND BRITISH POLITICS Allen and Unwin London 1962

Driver C P | THE DISARMERS Hodder and Stoughton London 1964

Eckstein H | PRESSURE GROUP POLITICS: THE CASE OF THE BRITISH MEDICAL ASSOCIATION Allen and Unwin London 1960

Finer S E   ANONYMOUS EMPIRE: A STUDY OF THE LOBBY IN
                             GREAT BRITAIN Pall Mall Press London 1958

Finer S E   'The federation of British Industries'
                             Political Studies February 1956

Finer S E   'The political power of private capital'
                             Sociological Review December 1955 and
                             July 1956

Hain Peter   DON'T PLAY WITH APARTHEID: THE BACKGROUND TO
                             THE STOP THE SEVENTIES TOUR Allen and Unwin
                             London 1971

Heinemann Benjamin W   THE POLITICS OF THE POWERLESS: A STUDY OF THE
                             CAMPAIGN AGAINST RACIAL DISCRIMINATION Oxford
                             University Press London 1972

McKenzie R T   'Parties, Pressure Groups and the British
                             political process' Political Quarterly
                             January - March 1958 (special number on
                             Pressure Groups)

Mackenzie W S M   'Pressure groups: the conceptual framework'
                             Political Studies October 1955

McKie David   A SADLY MISMANAGED AFFAIR: A POLITICAL HISTORY
                             OF THE THIRD AIRPORT Croom Helm London 1974

Parkin F   MIDDLE CLASS RADICALISM: THE SOCIAL BASES
                             OF THE BRITISH CAMPAIGN FOR NUCLEAR DIS-
                             ARMAMENT Manchester University Press Manchester
                             1968

Potter A   ORGANISED GROUPS IN BRITISH NATIONAL POLITICS
                             Faber London 1961

Self P   THE STATE AND THE FARMER Allen and Unwin Lon-
                             don 1962

Simms Madeline and Hindell   ABORTION LAW REFORMED Peter Owen London 1971
Keith

Stewart J D   BRITISH PRESSURE GROUPS: THEIR ROLE IN RELA-
                             TION TO THE HOUSE OF COMMONS Oxford University
                             Press London 1958

Wilson H H   PRESSURE GROUP: THE CAMPAIGN FOR COMMERCIAL
                             TELEVISION Secker and Warburg London 1961

Wootton G   THE POLITICS OF INFLUENCE: BRITISH EX-
                             SERVICEMEN, CABINET DECISIONS AND CULTURAL
                             EXCHANGE 1917-1959 Routledge and Kegan Paul
                             London 1963

G SOCIAL POLICY

(see also other sections for social policy in specific fields e g E Education
H 21 Health Service and B 43 Mid-nineteenth century social policy)

Abel-Smith Brian
Zander Michael and Brooke
Rosalind
LEGAL PROBLEMS AND THE CITIZEN Heinemann
London 1973

Atkinson A B
POVERTY IN BRITAIN AND THE REFORM OF SOCIAL
SECURITY Cambridge University Press London 1969

Bruce Maurice
THE COMING OF THE WELFARE STATE Batsford London 1961

Bruce Maurice ed
THE RISE OF THE WELFARE STATE: ENGLISH SOCIAL
POLICY 1601-1971 Weidenfeld and Nicolson
London 1973

Cooper Michael H
SOCIAL POLICY: A SURVEY OF RECENT DEVELOPMENTS
Blackwell Oxford 1973

Davies B P
SOCIAL NEEDS AND RESOURCES IN LOCAL SERVICES
Michael Joseph London 1968

Davies Bleddyn et al
VARIATIONS IN CHILDREN'S SERVICES AMONG
BRITISH URBAN AUTHORITIES Bell London 1972

Davies Bleddyn et al
VARIATIONS IN SERVICES FOR THE AGED Bell
London 1971

European Journal of
Sociology
Special issue on 'Welfare State' 1961

Fisher A G B
ECONOMIC PROGRESS AND SOCIAL SECURITY Macmillan London 1945

Forder Anthony ed
PENELOPE HALL'S SOCIAL SERVICES OF ENGLAND
AND WALES Routledge and Kegan Paul London 1971

Friedmann W G
LAW AND SOCIAL CHANGE IN CONTEMPORARY BRITAIN
Stevens and Sons London 1951

George Victor
SOCIAL SECURITY: BEVERIDGE AND AFTER Routledge
and Kegan Paul London 1968

George Victor
SOCIAL SECURITY AND SOCIETY Routledge and
Kegan Paul London 1973

Gilbert Bentley B
BRITISH SOCIAL POLICY 1914-1939 Batsford
London 1970

Ginsberg M ed
LAW AND OPINION IN THE 20TH CENTURY Stevens
London 1959

Glass D V
'The application of social research' British
Journal of Sociology 1(1) 1950

Harris Josy	UNEMPLOYMENT AND POLITICS: A STUDY OF ENGLISH SOCIAL POLICY 1886-1914 Oxford University Press London 1972
Heclo Hugh	FROM RELIEF TO INCOME MAINTENANCE: MODERN SOCIAL POLICY-MAKING IN BRITAIN AND SWEDEN Yale University Press New Haven 1974
Heidenheimer Arnold J	'The politics of public education health and welfare in the USA and Western Europe: how growth and reform potentials have differed' British Journal of Political Science 3 (1973) 315-340
Herman Melvin	ADMINISTRATIVE JUSTICE AND SUPPLEMENTARY BENE-FITS Bell London 1972
Hill D ed (Nuffield Provincial Hospitals Trust)	THE BURDEN ON THE COMMUNITY Oxford University Press London 1962
Jones Kathleen ed	THE YEAR BOOK OF SOCIAL POLICY IN BRITAIN 1971 Routledge and Kegan Paul London 1972
Jones Kathleen ed	THE YEAR BOOK OF SOCIAL POLICY IN BRITAIN 1972 Routledge and Kegan Paul London 1973
Jordan Bill	POOR PARENTS: SOCIAL POLICY AND THE 'CYCLE OF DEPRIVATION' Routledge and Kegan Paul London 1974
Jordan Bill	PAUPERS: THE MAKING OF THE NEW CLAIMING CLASS Routledge and Kegan Paul London 1973
Kaim-Caudle P R	COMPARATIVE SOCIAL POLICY AND SOCIAL SECURITY: A TEN COUNTRY STUDY Martin Robertson London 1973
Kincaid I C	POVERTY AND EQUALITY IN BRITAIN: A STUDY OF SOCIAL SECURITY AND TAXATION Penguin Harmondsworth 1973
Lees Ray et al	POLITICS AND SOCIAL WORK Routledge and Kegan Paul London 1972
Lister R	AS MAN AND WIFE: A STUDY OF THE COHABITATION RULE Child Poverty Action Group London 1972
Lynes T	NATIONAL ASSISTANCE AND NATIONAL PROSPERITY Codicote Press Welwyn 1962
Meacher M	RATE REBATES: A STUDY OF THE EFFECTIVENESS OF MEANS TESTS Child Poverty Action Group London 1972
Marshall T H	SOCIAL POLICY Hutchinson University Library London 1970

Mayer John E and Timms Noel   THE CLIENT SPEAKS Routledge and Kegan Paul
                               London 1970

Peacock A   'The welfare society' in Watson G ed THE UN-
                               SERVILE STATE Allen and Unwin 1957

Pinker R A   SOCIAL THEORY AND SOCIAL POLICY Heinemann
                               London 1971

Political Quarterly   Vol 40 no 1 1969 special issue on the future
                               of the social services

Richardson J   ECONOMIC AND FINANCIAL ASPECTS OF SOCIAL SECU-
                               RITY Allen and Unwin London 1960

Rose Hilary   'Up against the welfare state: the claimants
                               unions' in Miliband R and Saville J eds
                               SOCIALIST REGISTER 1973 Merlin Press London
                               1973

Rose Michael F   THE ENGLISH POOR LAW 1780-1930 David and Charles
                               Newton Abbot 1971

Schonfeld Andrew and   SOCIAL INDICATORS AND SOCIAL POLICY Heinemann
Shaw Stella   London 1972

Schweinitz K de   ENGLAND'S ROAD TO SOCIAL SECURITY Oxford Uni-
                               versity Press London 1943 (new ed Barnes New
                               York 1961)

Simey T S   PRINCIPLES OF SOCIAL ADMINISTRATION Oxford Uni-
                               versity Press London 1937

Stephenson Olive   CLAIMANT OR CLIENT Allen and Unwin London 1972

Titmuss R M   COMMITMENT TO WELFARE Allen and Unwin London
                               1968

Titmuss R M   ESSAYS ON THE WELFARE STATE Allen and Unwin
                               London 1958

Titmuss R M   PROBLEMS OF SOCIAL POLICY Longmans London 1950

Townsend Peter et al   SOCIAL SERVICES FOR ALL? Fabian Society London
                               1968

Townsend Peter   'Scope and limitations of means-tested social
                               services in Britain' Transactions of the Man-
                               chester Statistical Society 1972

United Kingdom   SOCIAL INSURANCE AND ALLIED SERVICES (Beveridge
                               Report) (cmnd 6404) B P P 1942-3 vol II

United Kingdom: Committee   REPORT (cmnd 5228) HMSO London 1973
on Abuse of Social Security
Benefits

Webb B   MY APPRENTICESHIP Longmans London 1950

Webb B   DIARIES 1912-24 Cole Margaret ed Longmans
                                    London 1952

Webb B   DIARIES 1924-32 Cole Margaret ed Longmans
                                    London 1956

Webb S and B   ENGLISH POOR LAW POLICY 1910 Reprinted in
                                    ENGLISH LOCAL GOVERNMENT Vol 10: ENGLISH
                                    POOR LAW POLICY Cass London 1963

Wedderburn D   'Facts and theories of the welfare state' in
                                    Miliband R and Saville J eds SOCIALIST
                                    REGISTER 1965 Merlin Press London 1965

Wraith R E and Hutchinson   ADMINISTRATIVE TRIBUNALS Allen and Unwin
R G   London 1973

H POPULATION, FAMILY AND SPECIFIC DEMOGRAPHIC GROUPS
(see also J 20 Internal migration I 10 Immigration and Emigration :
general)

H 10 Population: General

Benjamin Bernard   THE POPULATION CENSUS: A SSRC REVIEW
Heinemann London 1970

British Association for the Symposium report no 4: 'Biosocial
Advancement of Science   aspects of life in Britain' Journal of
Biosocial Science Vol 5 No 2 April 1973

Carrier N H   'Demographic aspects of an ageing population' in Welford A T et al ed: SOCIETY
Routledge and Kegan Paul London 1962

Davis K   'The theory of change and response in modern
demographic history' Population Index 29(4)
October 1963

Drake M ed   POPULATION IN INDUSTRIALIZATION Methuen
London 1969

Flinn M W   BRITISH POPULATION GROWTH 1700-1850 Macmillan
London 1970

Glass D V and Eversley D   POPULATION IN HISTORY Edward Arnold London
eds   1965

Hollingsworth T H   THE DEMOGRAPHY OF THE BRITISH PEERAGE (Supplement to Population Studies 18(2) Nov 1964)

Kelsall R K   POPULATION Longman London 1967 Revised 1970

Population Investigation   TOWARDS A POPULATION POLICY FOR THE UNITED
Committee London School   KINGDOM (Supplement to Population Studies
of Economics   Vol 24 May 1970)

United Kingdom: Royal   REPORT (Cmnd 7695) HMSO London 1949
Commission on Population

United Kingdom: The   STATISTICAL REVIEW OF ENGLAND AND WALES
Registrar General's   Published annually

United Kingdom: Office   CENSUSES OF POPULATION: REPORTS Decenially
of Censuses and Surveys   (except 1941); latest full census 1971
(General Register Office   (sample census 1966)
England and Wales; Gene-
ral Registry Office Scot-
land)

United Kingdom: Population   REPORT (Cmnd 5258) HMSO London 1973
Panel

United Kingdom   LONG TERM POPULATION DISTRIBUTION IN GREAT
BRITAIN - A STUDY HMSO London 1971

H 20 Mortality and Morbidity

Butler N R and Bonham D G — PERINATAL MORTALITY Livingstone London 1963

Douglas J W B and Blomfield J M — CHILDREN UNDER FIVE George Allen London 1958

Forsyth G and Logan R — THE DEMAND FOR MEDICAL CARE Oxford University Press London 1960

Hair P E H — 'Deaths from Violence in Britain: a tentative secular survey' Population Studies 24(1) Jan 1971

Howe Melvyn — NATIONAL ATLAS OF DISEASE MORTALITY IN THE UNITED KINGDOM Nelson London 1970

Illsley R — 'Social class selection and class differences in relation to stillbirths and infant deaths' British Medical Journal Dec 24 1955

Logan W P D — 'Mortality in England and Wales from 1848 to 1947' Population Studies 4(2) Sept 1950

McKeown T M and Record R G — 'Reasons for the decline of mortality in England and Wales during the 19th century' Population Studies 16(2) Nov 1962 (Also in Glass and Eversley ed POPULATION IN HISTORY Edward Arnold London 1965)

Meade J E and Parkes A S eds — BIOLOGICAL ASPECTS OF SOCIAL PROBLEMS Oliver and Boyd Edinburgh 1965

Miller F J W et al — GROWING UP IN NEWCASTLE-UPON-TYNE Oxford University Press London 1960 (see also Spence Sir J)

Morris J N — USES OF EPIDEMIOLOGY E and S Livingstone Edinburgh and London 1957 (2nd ed 1964)

Morris J N and Heady J A — 'Social and biological factors in infant mortality' The Lancet 1955 12, 19 and 26 Feb 5 and 12 March

Peller S — 'Studies in mortality since the Renaissance' Bulletin of the History of Medicine XXI 1947

Platt R and Parkes A S eds — SOCIAL AND GENETIC INFLUENCES ON LIFE AND DEATH Oliver and Boyd Edinburgh 1968

Sociological Review — Monograph no 5 July 1962 on sociology and medicine

Susser M W and Watson W — SOCIOLOGY IN MEDICINE Oxford University Press London 1962

Spence Sir J et al

A THOUSAND FAMILIES IN NEWCASTLE-UPON-TYNE
AN APPROACH TO THE STUDY OF HEALTH AND ILL-
NESS IN CHILDREN Oxford University Press
London 1954 (see also Miller F J W)

Titmuss R M

BIRTH POVERTY AND WEALTH Hamish Hamilton London 1943

United Kingdom: General
Register Office

THE REGISTRAR-GENERAL'S DECENNIAL SUPPLEMENT
ENGLAND AND WALES 1951 OCCUPATION MORTALITY:
Part I 1954 (DECENNIAL SUPPLEMENT FOR 1961:
OCCUPATIONAL MORTALITY 1970)

United Kingdom: Ministry
of Pensions and National
Insurance

REPORT OF AN ENQUIRY INTO THE INCIDENCE OF
INCAPACITY FOR WORK (2 parts) 1964-65

United Kingdom: Registrar
General of Births Marriages
and Deaths

STUDIES IN MEDICAL AND POPULATION SUBJECTS

No 2 SICKNESS IN THE POPULATION OF ENGLAND
AND WALES 1944-47 (Stocks P) 1949

No 10 TUBERCULOSIS STATISTICS FOR ENGLAND
AND WALES 1938-55 (Logan W P D)

No 12 THE SURVEY OF SICKNESS 1943-52 (Logan
W P D and Brooke E M) 1957

No 13 CANCER STATISTICS FOR ENGLAND AND WALES
1901-55 (Mackenzie et al) 1957

No 14 MORBIDITY STATISTICS (Logan W P D and
Cushion A A) 2 vols 1958-60

No 15 SOCIAL AND BIOLOGICAL FACTORS IN IN-
FANT MORTALITY (Heady J A and Hearsman M A)

No 19 REGIONAL AND SOCIAL FACTORS IN IN-
FANT MORTALITY (Spicer CC and Lipworth L)
1966

See also:

Section H 10 Registrar-General's Statistical
Review

Section H 30 Royal Commission : Report and
Papers vol 4

Section H 30 Royal College of Obstetricians

H 21 Health services and medical practice
(see also G Social policy)

Abel-Smith B

THE HOSPITALS 1800-1948 Heinemann London 1964

Abel-Smith B and Titmuss R

THE COST OF THE NATIONAL HEALTH SERVICE
Cambridge University Press London 1956

Ashford J R and Pearson N G 'Who uses the Health Services and Why?' <u>Journal of the Royal Statistical Society</u> Series A (General) vol 133 part 3 1970

Braithwaite W J   LLOYD GEORGE'S AMBULANCE WAGON Methuen London 1957

Brown R G S   THE CHANGING NATIONAL HEALTH SERVICE Routledge and Kegan Paul London 1973

Butler J R et al   FAMILY DOCTORS AND PUBLIC POLICY Routledge and Kegan Paul London 1974

Cartwright A   PATIENTS AND THEIR DOCTORS: A STUDY OF GENERAL PRACTICE Routledge and Kegan Paul London 1967

Eckstein H   THE ENGLISH HEALTH SERVICE Harvard University Press Cambridge Mass 1958

Ferguson T et al   PUBLIC HEALTH AND URBAN GROWTH University College Centre for Urban Studies London 1964

Honigsbaum Frank   THE STRUGGLE FOR THE MINISTRY OF HEALTH Bell London 1971

Jewkes J and S   THE GENESIS OF THE BRITISH NATIONAL HEALTH SERVICE Blackwell Oxford 1960

Jones Kathleen   MENTAL HEALTH AND SOCIAL POLICY 1845-1959 Routledge and Kegan Paul London 1960

Jones Kathleen   A HISTORY OF THE MENTAL HEALTH SERVICE Routledge and Kegan Paul London 1972

Lindsay A   SOCIALIZED MEDICINE IN ENGLAND AND WALES: THE NATIONAL HEALTH SERVICE 1948-1961 Oxford University Press London 1962

Logan R F L Ashley J S A Klein R E Robson D M   DYNAMICS OF MEDICAL CARE: THE LIVERPOOL STUDY INTO THE USE OF HOSPITAL RESOURCES William Dawson London 1972

McKeown T   MEDICINE IN MODERN SOCIETY Allen and Unwin London 1965

Pinker R   ENGLISH HOSPITAL STATISTICS 1861-1938 Heinemann London 1966

Titmuss Richard M   THE GIFT RELATIONSHIP Allen and Unwin London 1971

United Kingdom: Committee of Enquiry into the Cost of the National Health Service   REPORT (Cmnd 9663) HMSO London 1956

United Kingdom: Department of Health and Social Security	NATIONAL HEALTH SERVICE REORGANIZATION: ENGLAND (Cmnd 5055) HMSO London 1972
Willcocks A J	THE CREATION OF THE NATIONAL HEALTH SERVICE Routledge and Kegan Paul London 1967

H 30 Fertility and family size

Banks J A	PROSPERITY AND PARENTHOOD Routledge and Kegan Paul London 1954
Banks J A and O	FEMINISM AND FAMILY PLANNING IN VICTORIAN ENGLAND Liverpool University Press Liverpool 1964
Berent J	'Fertility and social mobility' Population Studies 5(3) March 1952
Carlsson G	'The decline of fertility: innovation or adjustment process' Population Studies 20(2) November 1966
Chou R-C and Brown S	'A comparison of the size of families of Roman Catholics and Non-Catholics in Great Britain' Population Studies 22(1) March 1968
Eversley D E C	SOCIAL THEORIES OF FERTILITY AND THE MALTHUSIAN DEBATE Oxford University Press London 1959
Fryer P	THE BIRTH CONTROLLERS Secker and Warburg London 1965
Glass D V	'Family limitation in Europe: a survey of recent studies' in Kiser C V ed RESEARCH IN FAMILY PLANNING Princeton University Press Princeton N J 1962
Glass D V	'Family planning programmes and action in Western Europe' Population Studies 19(3) March 1966
Glass D V	'Fertility trends in Europe since the Second World War' Population Studies 21(3) March 1968
Glass D V	POPULATION: POLICIES AND MOVEMENTS IN EUROPE Frank Cass London 1967 (see especially Ch 1)
Glass D V ed	INTRODUCTION TO MALTHUS Watts London 1953
Hajnal J and Henderson A M	'The economic position of the family' Papers of the Royal Commission on Population Vol 5 HMSO London 1950
Hawthorn Geoffrey	THE SOCIOLOGY OF FERTILITY Collier/Macmillan London 1970

Hollingsworth T H   THE DEMOGRAPHY OF THE BRITISH PEERAGE London School of Economics Population Investigation Committee London 1965

Horobin Gordon ed   EXPERIENCE WITH ABORTION: A CASE STUDY OF NORTH EAST SCOTLAND Cambridge University Press London 1973

Johnson G   'Differential fertility in European countries' in Universities National Bureau Committee for Economic Research: DEMOGRAPHIC AND ECONOMIC CHANGE IN DEVELOPED COUNTRIES Oxford University Press London 1961

Matras J   'Social strategies of family formation: data for British female cohorts born 1831-1906' Population Studies 19(2) November 1965

Micklewright F H A   'The rise and decline of English Neo-Malthusianism' Population Studies 1961

Maxwell J   SOCIAL IMPLICATION OF THE 1947 SCOTTISH MENTAL SURVEY University of London Press London 1953

Peel J   'The Hull Family survey. I: The survey couples 1966' Journal of Biosocial Science 2(1) January 1970

Peel J   'The Hull Family survey. II: Family planning in the first five years of marriage' Journal of Biosocial Science vol 4 no 3 July 1972

Penrose L S   PROBLEM OF INTELLIGENCE AND HEREDITY London 1959

Rowntree G and Pierce R M   'Birth control in Britain' Population Studies July and November 1961

Royal College of Obstetricians and Gynaecologists and Population Investigation Joint Committee   MATERNITY IN GREAT BRITAIN Oxford University Press London 1948

Scottish Council for Research in Education: Mental Survey Committee   EDUCATIONAL AND OTHER ASPECTS OF THE 1947 SCOTTISH MENTAL SURVEY University of London Press London 1958

Thompson B and Illsley R   'Family growth in Aberdeen' Journal of Biosocial Science 1(1) January 1969

Thomson G H   THE TREND OF SCOTTISH INTELLIGENCE 1949

Titmuss R M and K   PARENTS REVOLT Secker and Warburg London 1942

United Kingdom: Royal Committee on Population   REPORT (Cmnd 7695) HMSO London 1949

United Kingdom: Royal Commission on Population — PAPERS vol 1 REPORT OF ENQUIRY INTO FAMILY LIMITATIONS... by Lewis-Faning E HMSO London 1949

United Kingdom: Royal Commission on Population — PAPERS vol 3 THE ECONOMIC CONSEQUENCES OF THE PRESENT TREND OF POPULATION. REPORT OF THE ECONOMIC COMMITTEE HMSO London 1950

United Kingdom: Royal Commission on Population — PAPERS vol 4 REPORTS OF THE BIOLOGICAL AND MEDICAL COMMITTEE HMSO London 1950

United Kingdom: Royal Commission on Population — PAPERS vol 6 THE TREND AND PATTERN OF FERTILITY IN GREAT BRITAIN: REPORT ON THE FAMILY CENSUS OF 1946 by Glass D V and Grebenik E HMSO London 1954

Woolf Myra — FAMILY INTENTIONS United Kingdom Office of Population Censuses and Surveys Social Survey Division HMSO London 1971

Wrong D — 'Class fertility differences in England and Wales' Millbank Memorial Fund Quarterly January 1960

H 40 Marriage

Dixon Ruth B — 'Explaining cross-cultural variations in age at marriage and proportions never marrying' Population Studies 25(2) July 1971

Glass D V ed — SOCIAL MOBILITY IN BRITAIN Routledge and Kegan Paul London 1954 (see Ch XII)

Gorer G — EXPLORING ENGLISH CHARACTER Cresset Press London 1955 (see ch IX and X)

Gorer G — SEX AND MARRIAGE IN ENGLAND TODAY Nelson London 1971

Grebenik E and Rowntree G — 'Factors associated with age at marriage in Britain' Proc Royal Society Series B 159 10 December 1963

Hajnal J — 'Age at marriage and proportions marrying' Population Studies 7(2) November 1953

Hajnal J — 'European marriage patterns in perspective' in Glass D V and Eversley D E C eds. POPULATION IN HISTORY Edward Arnold London 1965

Pierce R M — 'Marriage in the "fifties"' Sociological Review 11(2) July 1963

Slater E and Woodside M — PATTERNS OF MARRIAGE Cassell London 1951

H 50 Family and kinship: general

Anderson Michael — FAMILY STRUCTURE IN NINETEENTH CENTURY LANCA-SHIRE Cambridge University Press London 1971

Anderson Michael ed — THE SOCIOLOGY OF THE FAMILY Penguin Harmondsworth 1971

Arensberg C — THE IRISH COUNTRYMAN Macmillan London 1937

Beales H L — 'The Victorian family' in Grisewood H IDEAS AND BELIEFS OF THE VICTORIANS BBC Publications 1949

Bell C R — MIDDLE CLASS FAMILIES: SOCIAL AND GEOGRAPHICAL MOBILITY Routledge and Kegan Paul London 1968

Bell Lady F E E — AT THE WORKS: A STUDY OF A MANUFACTURING TOWN Edward Arnold London 1907 Nelson London 1911

Bott E — FAMILY AND SOCIAL NETWORK Tavistock Press London 1957 (2nd ed 1971)

Farmer M — THE FAMILY Longmans London 1969

Firth R ed — TWO STUDIES OF KINSHIP IN LONDON Athlone Press London 1957

Firth R et al — FAMILIES AND THEIR RELATIVES Routledge and Kegan Paul London 1970

Fletcher R — THE FAMILY AND MARRIAGE Penguin Harmondsworth 1962 (revised ed 1966)

Gibson Colin — 'The Association between divorces and social class in England and Wales' British Journal of Sociology vol 25(1) March 1974

Glass R and Davidson F G — 'Household structure and housing needs' Population Studies 4(4) March 1951

Goldthorpe J H et al — THE AFFLUENT WORKER IN THE CLASS STRUCTURE Cambridge University Press London 1969

Goode W J et al — 'The sociology of the family (Opatija seminar) the impact of urbanization and industrialization on the family' Current Sociology 12(1) 1963-64 (see e g contributions by Goode W J and Klein V)

Harris C C — READINGS IN KINSHIP IN URBAN SOCIETY Pergamon Press Oxford 1970

Kelsall R Keith Poole Anne Kuhn Annette — 'Marriage and family-building patterns of university graduates' Journal of Biosocial Science vol 3 no 3 July 1971

Laslett P — 'Size and structure of the household in England over three centuries' Population Studies 23(2) July 1969

McGregor O R   DIVORCE IN ENGLAND: A CENTENARY STUDY Heinemann
                                London 1957

Marris P   WIDOWS AND THEIR FAMILIES Routledge and Kegan
                                Paul London 1958

Mills E   LIVING WITH MENTAL ILLNESS Routledge and Kegan
                                Paul London 1962

Mogey J M   FAMILY AND NEIGHBOURHOOD Oxford University
                                Press London 1956

Pohl J M and R E   MANAGERS AND THEIR WIVES Allen Lane London 1971

Platt J   'Some problems in measuring the jointness of
                                conjugal role-relationships' Sociology 3(3)
                                September 1969

Reeves M S   ROUND ABOUT A POUND A WEEK G Bell and Son London
                                1913

Rice M Spring   WORKING CLASS WIVES: THEIR HEALTH AND CONDITIONS
                                Penguin Harmondsworth 1939

Rosser C and Harris C   THE FAMILY AND SOCIAL CHANGE: A STUDY OF FAMILY
                                AND KINSHIP IN A SOUTH WALES TOWN Routledge
                                and Kegan Paul London 1966

Smelser N   SOCIAL CHANGE IN THE INDUSTRIAL REVOLUTION
                                Routledge and Kegan Paul London 1959

Stacey M   TRADITION AND CHANGE: A STUDY OF BANBURY
                                Oxford University Press London 1960

Titmuss R M   'The family as a social institution' in his
                                ESSAYS ON THE WELFARE STATE Allen and Unwin
                                London 1958

Willmott P   'Kinship and social legislation' British Journal
                                of Sociology 1958

Willmott P   THE EVOLUTION OF A COMMUNITY Routledge and Kegan
                                Paul London 1963

Young M D   'Distribution of income within the family'
                                British Journal of Sociology 3(4) December 1952

Young M and Willmott P   FAMILY AND CLASS IN A LONDON SUBURB Routledge
                                and Kegan Paul London 1960

Young M and Willmott P   FAMILY AND KINSHIP IN EAST LONDON Routledge
                                and Kegan Paul London 1957

Young M and Willmott P   THE SYMMETRICAL FAMILY: A STUDY OF WORK AND
                                LEISURE IN A LONDON REGION Routledge and Kegan
                                Paul London 1973

Platt J   SOCIAL RESEARCH IN BETHNAL GREEN: AN EVALU-
                                ATION OF THE WORK OF THE INSTITUTE OF COM-
                                MUNITY STUDIES Macmillan London 1971

H 60 Stability of the family

Archbishop of Canterbury's Group on the Divorce Law	PUTTING ASUNDER (Mortimer Report) HMSO London 1964
Carrier N H and Rowntree G	'The resort to divorce in England and Wales 1858-1957' Population Studies March 1958
Eekelaar John	FAMILY SECURITY AND FAMILY BREAKDOWN Penguin Harmondsworth 1971
Lee B H	DIVORCE LAW REFORM IN ENGLAND Peter Owen London 1974
McGregor O R	DIVORCE IN ENGLAND Heinemann London 1957
McGregor O R Blom-Cooper L and Gibson C	SEPARATED SPOUSES Duckworth London 1971
Morris P	PRISONERS AND THEIR FAMILIES Allen and Unwin London 1965
Rowntree G	'Some aspects of marriage breakdown' Population Studies November 1961
Rowntree G	'Early childhood in broken families' Population Studies VIII(3) March 1955
Rowntree G	'Some aspects of marriage breakdown in Britain during the last thirty years' Population Studies 18(2) November 1964
United Kingdom: Royal Commission on Divorce and Matrimonial Causes	REPORT (Cmnd 6478) 1912 B P P 1912-13 XVIII MINUTES OF EVIDENCE AND APPENDICES 1912-13 XVIII XIX and XX HMSO London
United Kingdom: Royal Commission on Marriage and Divorce	REPORT 1951-1955 (Cmnd 9678) 1956 MINUTES OF EVIDENCE APPENDIX AND INDEX 1952-56 HMSO London

H 70 The position and employment of women

Douglas J W B and Bloomfield J	CHILDREN UNDER FIVE Allen and Unwin London 1958
Fogarty Michael Allen A J Allen Isobel and Walters P	WOMEN IN TOP JOBS Allen and Unwin London 1971
Fogarty Michael and Rapoport Rhona and Robert	SEX, CAREER AND FAMILY Allen and Unwin London 1971
Gavron H	THE CAPTIVE WIFE Routledge and Kegan Paul London 1966

Hewitt M — WIVES AND MOTHERS IN VICTORIAN INDUSTRY Rockliff London 1958

Hubback J — WIVES WHO WENT TO COLLEGE Heinemann London 1957

Hunt A — A SURVEY OF WOMEN'S EMPLOYMENT (2 vols) HMSO London 1968

James E — 'Women at work in 20th century Britain' Manchester School September 1962

Jephcott P et al — MARRIED WOMEN WORKING Allen and Unwin London 1962

Kelsall R K — WOMEN AND TEACHING HMSO London 1963

Kelsall R K and Mitchell S — 'Married women and employment in England and Wales' Population Studies 13(1) July 1959

Klein V — BRITAIN'S MARRIED WOMEN WORKERS Routledge and Kegan Paul London 1965

Klein V — WOMEN WORKERS: WORKING HOURS AND SERVICES Organisation for Economic Cooperation and Development London 1965

Klein V — EMPLOYING MARRIED WOMEN Institute of Personnel Management London 1961

Klein V — THE FEMININE CHARACTER Routledge and Kegan Paul London 1946

Klein V — WORKING WIVES Institute of Personnel Management London 1960

McGregor O R — 'The social position of women in England 1850-1914: a bibliography' British Journal of Sociology 6(1) March 1955

McGregor O R — 'Equality, sexual values and permissive legislation: the English experience' Journal of Social Policy vol 1 part 1 January 1972

Mackay Ann Wilding Paul and George Vic — 'Stereotypes of male and female roles and their influence on people's attitudes to one parent families' Sociological Review vol 20 no 1 February 1972

Mitchell Juliet — WOMEN'S ESTATE Penguin Harmondsworth 1971

Myrdal A and Klein V — WOMEN'S TWO ROLES: HOME AND WORK Routledge and Kegan Paul London 1956

Oakley Ann — SEX GENDER AND SOCIETY Maurice Temple Smith London 1972

Pinchbeck I   WOMEN WORKERS AND THE INDUSTRIAL REVOLUTION
1750-1850 G Routledge and Sons London 1930

Political and Economic   WOMEN IN TOP JOBS PEP London 1971
Planning (PEP)   WOMEN AND TOP JOBS (interim report) PEP London 1967

Rapoport Rhona and Robert   DUAL CAREER FAMILIES Penguin Harmondsworth 1971

Reiss E   RIGHTS AND DUTIES OF ENGLISHWOMEN: A STUDY IN
LAW AND PUBLIC OPINION Sherratt and Hughes
Manchester 1934

Rowbotham Sheila   WOMEN'S CONSCIOUSNESS, MAN'S WORLD Penguin
Harmondsworth 1973

Rowbotham Sheila   HIDDEN FROM HISTORY Pluto London 1973

Rowbotham Sheila   RESISTANCE AND REVOLUTION Allen and Unwin
London 1972

Strachey R   THE CAUSE: A SHORT HISTORY OF THE WOMEN'S MOVE-
MENT IN GREAT BRITAIN G Bell and Son London
1928

Walters P Allen A J and   WOMEN IN TOP JOBS Allen and Unwin London 1971
Allen I

Yudkin S and Holme A   WORKING MOTHERS AND THEIR CHILDREN Michael
Joseph London 1963

Zweig F   WOMEN'S LIFE AND LABOUR Gollancz London 1952

H 80   Childhood and youth
(see also E Education)
H 80   Childhood

Davie Ronald Butler Neville   FROM BIRTH TO SEVEN Longmans London 1972
and Goldstein Harvey

National Child Development   11,000 SEVEN YEAR OLDS Longmans London 1966
Study (1958 Cohort)

Newson J and E   PATTERNS OF INFANT CARE IN AN URBAN COMMUNITY
Penguin Harmondsworth 1965
FOUR YEARS OLD IN URBAN COMMUNITY Allen and
Unwin London 1968
(see also 'Some social differences in the pro-
cess of child rearing' in Gould S J ed PENGUIN
SOCIAL SCIENCES SURVEY 1968 Penguin Harmonds-
worth 1968)

Pinchbeck Ivy and Hewitt   CHILDREN IN ENGLISH SOCIETY: vol 2 FROM 18TH
Margaret   CENTURY TO THE CHILDREN'S ACT 1948 Routledge
and Kegan Paul London 1974

Spinley B M   THE DEPRIVED AND THE PRIVILEGED Routledge and
               Kegan Paul London 1953

Wedge P and Prosser H   BORN TO FAIL Arow London 1973
                         (Follow up of National Child Development study)

H 81 Youth
(see also K 31 Juvenile delinquency and L 10 Culture and leisure: general)

Abrams P and Little A N   'The young voter in British politics; the
                           young activist in British politics' British
                           Journal of Sociology 16(2 and 4) June and
                           December 1965

Carter M P   HOME, SCHOOL AND WORK Pergamon Press Oxford
              1962

Emmett Isabel   YOUTH AND LEISURE IN AN URBAN SPRAWL
                 Manchester University Press Manchester 1971

Eppel E M and M   ADOLESCENTS AND MORALITY Routledge and Kegan
                   Paul London 1966

Ferguson T and Cunnison J   THE YOUNG WAGE-EARNER; A STUDY OF GLASGOW
                             BOYS 1951 Oxford University Press London 1951
                             Also: id IN THEIR EARLY TWENTIES: A STUDY OF
                             GLASGOW YOUTH Oxford University Press London
                             1956

Jephcott A P   GIRLS GROWING UP Faber London 1949

Jephcott A P   RISING TWENTY Faber London 1948

Keele E T   'Youth and Work' Sociological Review 14(2)
            1966

Leigh John   YOUNG PEOPLE AND LEISURE Routledge and Kegan
             Paul London 1971

Mays J B   THE YOUNG PRETENDERS Michael Joseph London
           1965

Mills Richard   YOUNG OUTSIDERS: A STUDY OF ALTERNATIVE COM-
                MUNITIES Routledge and Kegan Paul London 1973

Milson Fred   'Social origins of full-time youth leaders'
              Sociological Review 14(2) 1966

Milson Fred   YOUTH IN A CHANGING SOCIETY Routledge and Kegan
               Paul London 1972

Musgrove F   YOUTH AND THE SOCIAL ORDER Routledge and Kegan
             Paul London 1964

Paterson A   ACROSS THE BRIDGES OR LIFE BY THE SOUTH LONDON RIVERSIDE Edward Arnold London 1911

Patrick James   A GLASGOW GANG OBSERVED Eyre Methuen London 1973

Raison T ed   YOUTH IN NEW SOCIETY Hart Davies London 1966

Schofield Michael   THE SEXUAL BEHAVIOUR OF YOUNG PEOPLE Longmans London 1965 (revised 1968)

Schofield Michael   THE SEXUAL BEHAVIOUR OF YOUNG ADULTS Allen Lane London 1973

Smith C S   ADOLESCENCE Longmans London 1968

Smith David M   'Adolescence: a study of stereotyping' Sociological Review vol 18 no 2 July 1970

United Kingdom: Committee on the age of majority   REPORT (Cmnd 3342) HMSO London 1967

Wilkins L T   THE ADOLESCENTS IN BRITAIN (Government Social Survey) HMSO London 1956

Willmott P   ADOLESCENT BOYS OF EAST LONDON Penguin Harmondsworth 1969 (revised ed)

H 90   Old age
(see also G Social policy)

Clark F leGros   WORK AGE AND LEISURE: CAUSES AND CONSEQUENCES OF THE SHORTENED WORKING LIFE Joseph London 1966

Cole D and Utting J E G   THE ECONOMIC CIRCUMSTANCES OF OLD PEOPLE Codicote Press Welwyn 1962

Harris Amelia I assisted by Clausen Rosemary   SOCIAL WELFARE FOR THE ELDERLY: A STUDY IN THIRTEEN LOCAL AUTHORITY AREAS IN ENGLAND WALES AND SCOTLAND vols I and II Government Social Survey HMSO London 1968

Ministry of Pensions and National Insurance   FINANCIAL AND OTHER CIRCUMSTANCES OF RETIREMENT PENSIONERS HMSO London 1966

Shanas E Townsend P Frus H et al   OLD PEOPLE IN THREE INDUSTRIAL SOCIETIES Routledge and Kegan Paul London 1968

Shenfield B   SOCIAL POLICIES FOR OLD AGE Routledge and Kegan Paul London 1957

Townsend P   THE LAST REFUGE Routledge and Kegan Paul London 1963

Townsend P   FAMILY LIFE OF OLD PEOPLE Routledge and Kegan
                          Paul London 1957

Townsend P   THE DEVELOPMENT OF HOME AND WELFARE SERVICES
                          FOR OLD PEOPLE 1946-60 Association of Directors
                          of Welfare Services Leicester 1961

Townsend P and Wedderburn D THE AGED IN THE WELFARE STATE (Occasional
                          Papers in Social Administration no 14) Bell
                          London 1965

Tunstall J   OLD AND ALONE Routledge and Kegan Paul London
                          1966

I EXTERNAL MIGRATION AND MINORITY GROUPS

I 10   Immigration and emigration: General
(see also H 10 Population: General)

Appleyard R T	BRITISH EMIGRATION TO AUSTRALIA Weidenfeld and Nicolson London 1965
Bechofer F ed	POPULATION GROWTH AND THE BRAIN DRAIN Edinburgh University Press Edinburgh 1969
Böhning W R	THE MIGRATION OF WORKERS IN THE UNITED KINGDOM AND THE EUROPEAN COMMUNITY Oxford University Press London 1972
Carrier N H and Jeffery J R	EXTERNAL MIGRATION: A STUDY OF THE AVAILABLE STATISTICS 1915–1950 (United Kingdom Registrar General: Studies on Medical and Population Subjects no 6) HMSO London 1953
Jackson J A ed	MIGRATION (Sociological Studies 2) Cambridge University Press London 1969
Thomas Brinley	MIGRATION AND URBAN DEVELOPMENT: A REAPPRAISAL OF BRITISH AND AMERICAN LONG CYCLES Methuen London 1972
United Kingdom: Royal Commission on Population	REPORT HMSO London 1949

I 20 Minority groups: General

Abbott Simon	THE PREVENTION OF RACIAL DISCRIMINATION IN BRITAIN Oxford University Press London 1971
Bagley Christopher	'Immigrant Children: a review of problems and policy in education' Journal of Social Policy vol 2 part 4 October 1973
Castles Stephen and Kosack Godula	IMMIGRANT WORKERS AND CLASS STRUCTURE IN WESTERN EUROPE Oxford University Press London 1973
Daniel W W	RACIAL DISCRIMINATION IN ENGLAND Penguin Harmondsworth 1968 (based on a PEP report) (see also Political and Economic Planning (PEP) and Research Services Ltd: RACIAL DISCRIMINATION PEP London 1967)
Dummett Ann	A PORTRAIT OF ENGLISH RACISM Penguin Harmondsworth 1973
Foot P	IMMIGRATION AND RACE IN BRITISH POLITICS Penguin Harmondsworth 1965

Glass R

'Insider-outsiders: the position of minorities'
Transactions, Fifth World Congress of Sociology vol III 1964

Hepple B

RACE, JOBS AND THE LAW IN BRITAIN Allen Lane
London 1968/Penguin Harmondsworth 1970

Hill Michael J and
Issacharoff R M

COMMUNITY ACTION AND RACE RELATIONS: A STUDY
OF COMMUNITY RELATIONS COMMITTEES IN BRITAIN
Oxford University Press London 1971

Krausz Ernest

ETHNIC MINORITIES IN BRITAIN MacGibbon and
Kee London 1971

Lester Anthony and Bindman
Geoffrey

RACE AND LAW Penguin Harmondsworth 1972

Lambert John R

CRIME, POLICE AND RACE RELATIONS: A STUDY IN
BIRMINGHAM Oxford University Press London 1970

Mason Philip

RACE RELATIONS Oxford University Press London
1970

Political and Economic
Planning (PEP)

ANTI-DISCRIMINATION LEGISLATION (Street Report)
PEP London 1967

Rex John

RACE, COLONIALISM AND THE CITY Routledge and
Kegan Paul London 1973

Rex John

RACE RELATIONS IN SOCIOLOGICAL THEORY
Weidenfeld and Nicolson London 1970

Runciman W G and Bagley
C R

'Status consistency, relative deprivation and
attitudes to immigrants' Sociology 3(3)
September 1969

Zubaida Sami ed

RACE AND RACIALISM Tavistock London 1970

I 30   Jews in Britain

Bermant Chaim

THE COUSIN-HOOD: THE ANGLO-JEWISH GENTRY Eyre
and Spottiswoode London 1971

Freedman M ed

A MINORITY IN BRITAIN Vallentine Mitchell and
Co London 1955

Gainer Bernhard

THE ALIEN INVASION Heinemann London 1972

Garrard John A

THE ENGLISH AND IMMIGRATION 1880-1910 A COM-
PARATIVE STUDY OF THE JEWISH INFLUX Oxford
University Press London 1971

Gartner L P

THE JEWISH IMMIGRANT IN ENGLAND 1870-1914
Allen and Unwin London 1960

Gould S J and Esh S ed	JEWISH LIFE IN MODERN BRITAIN Routledge and Kegan Paul London 1964
Krausz E	LEEDS JEWRY Heffers Cambridge 1964 (see also idem: A SOCIOLOGICAL FIELD STUDY OF JEWISH SUBURBAN LIFE IN EDGWARE 1962-63 1965 - unpublished Ph D thesis London School of Economics library)
Lipman V D	SOCIAL HISTORY OF THE JEWS IN ENGLAND 1850-1950 Watts London 1954
Lipman V D	A CENTURY OF SOCIAL SERVICE 1859-1959 Routledge and Kegan Paul London 1959
Lipman V D	'Trends in Anglo-Jewish occupations' Jewish Journal of Sociology 2(2) November 1960
Prais S J and Schmool Marlena	'The fertility of Jewish families in Britain 1971' Jewish Journal of Sociology vol XV no 2 December 1973
Sharf A	THE BRITISH PRESS AND JEWS UNDER NAZI RULE Oxford University Press London 1964
United Kingdom: Royal Commission on Alien Immigration	REPORT AND MINUTES OF EVIDENCE 4 vols (B P P 1903 IX)

I 40   Coloured minorities in Britain

Allen Sheila	NEW MINORITIES OLD CONFLICTS: ASIAN AND WEST INDIAN MIGRANTS IN GREAT BRITAIN Random House New York 1971
Bagley Christopher	SOCIAL STRUCTURE AND PREJUDICE IN FIVE ENGLISH BOROUGHS Institute of Race Relations London 1972
Banton M P	THE COLOURED QUARTER Jonathan Cape London 1955
Banton M P	RACE RELATIONS Tavistock London 1967 (see chapter on Britain)
Banton M P	WHITE AND COLOURED IN BRITAIN Jonathan Cape London 1959
Beetham David	TRANSPORT AND TURBANS: A COMPARATIVE STUDY IN LOCAL POLITICS Oxford University Press London 1970
Brooks Dennis	RACE AND LABOUR IN LONDON TRANSPORT Oxford University Press London 1973

Marsh P — THE ANATOMY OF A STRIKE: UNIONS, EMPLOYERS AND PUNJABI WORKERS IN A SOUTHALL FACTORY Institute of Race Relations special series Institute of Race Relations London 1968

Patterson S — DARK STRANGERS Penguin Harmondsworth 1965 (2nd ed)

Patterson S — IMMIGRATION AND RACE RELATIONS IN BRITAIN 1960-1967 Oxford University Press London 1969

Patterson S — IMMIGRANTS IN INDUSTRY Oxford University Press London 1968

Peach C — WEST INDIAN MIGRATION TO BRITAIN: A SOCIAL GEOGRAPHY Oxford University Press London 1968

Political and Economic Planning (PEP) — COLONIAL STUDENTS IN BRITAIN PEP London 1955

Rex J and Moore R — RACE COMMUNITY AND CONFLICT Oxford University Press London 1966

Richmond A H — COLOUR PREJUDICE IN BRITAIN: A STUDY OF WEST INDIAN WORKERS IN LIVERPOOL 1944-51 Routledge and Kegan Paul London 1954

Richmond A H — THE COLOUR PROBLEM Penguin Harmondsworth 1961

Richmond A H — MIGRATION AND RACE RELATIONS IN AN ENGLISH CITY: A STUDY IN BRISTOL Oxford University Press London 1973

Rimmer Malcolm — RACE AND INDUSTRIAL CONFLICT Heinemann London 1972

Rose E J B et al — COLOUR AND CITIZENSHIP: A REPORT ON BRITISH RACE RELATIONS Oxford University Press London 1968

Singh Amar Kumar — INDIAN STUDENTS IN BRITAIN Asia Publishing House Bombay and New York 1963

Survey of Race Relations in Britain (Deakin N ed) — COLOUR AND THE BRITISH ELECTORATE Pall Mall Press London 1965

Tajfel H and Dawson J L eds — DISAPPOINTED GUESTS Oxford University Press London 1965

United Kingdom: Select Committee on Race Relations and Immigration (House of Commons, Session 1968-69) — THE PROBLEMS OF COLOURED SCHOOL-LEAVERS vol I : REPORT HMSO London 1969

Wright P L — THE COLOURED WORKER IN BRITISH INDUSTRY WITH SPECIAL REFERENCE TO THE MIDLANDS AND NORTH OF ENGLAND Oxford University Press London 1968

I 50 Other immigrant minorities in Britain

Acton Thomas — GYPSY POLITICS AND SOCIAL CHANGE Routledge and Kegan Paul London 1974

Choo N K — THE CHINESE IN LONDON Oxford University Press London 1968

Jackson J A — THE IRISH IN BRITAIN Routledge and Kegan Paul London 1963 (see also idem in Centre for Urban Studies ed: LONDON — ASPECTS OF CHANGE Mac-Gibbon and Kee London 1964)

Oakley R — NEW BACKGROUNDS: THE IMMIGRANT CHILD AT HOME AND AT SCHOOL Oxford University Press London 1968

Patterson S — 'The Poles in London' in Centre for Urban Studies ed: LONDON — ASPECTS OF CHANGE Mac-Gibbon and Kee London 1964

Sandford Jeremy — GYPSIES Secker and Warburg London 1973

Tannahill J A — EUROPEAN VOLUNTEER WORKERS IN BRITAIN Manchester University Press Manchester 1958

United Kingdom: Sociological Research Section, Ministry of Housing and Local Government — GYPSIES AND OTHER TRAVELLERS HMSO London 1967

Zubrzycki J — POLISH IMMIGRANTS IN BRITAIN Nijhoff London 1956

J URBANISM AND RURAL COMMUNITIES

J 10   General

Ashworth W — THE GENESIS OF MODERN BRITISH TOWN PLANNING
Routledge and Kegan Paul London 1954

Centre for Urban Studies ed — LONDON: ASPECTS OF CHANGE MacGibbon and Kee
London 1964

Coates B E and E M Rawstron — REGIONAL VARIATIONS IN BRITAIN Batsford
London 1971

Dyos H J ed — THE STUDY OF URBAN HISTORY Edward Arnold
London 1968

Ferguson T et al — PUBLIC HEALTH AND URBAN GROWTH Centre for
Urban Studies London 1964

Frankenberg R — COMMUNITIES IN BRITAIN Penguin Harmondsworth
1966

Glass D V — THE TOWN AND CHANGING CIVILISATION John Lane
London 1935

Glass R — 'Urban sociology in Great Britain' Current
Sociology 4(4) 1955   Reprinted in part in
Pahl R E ed READINGS IN URBAN SOCIOLOGY
Pergamon Oxford 1968

Glass R — 'Urban sociology' in Welford A T et al ed
SOCIETY: PROBLEMS AND METHODS OF STUDY
Routledge and Kegan Paul London 1962

Mann P — AN APPROACH TO URBAN SOCIOLOGY   Routledge and
Kegan Paul London 1965

Morris R N — URBAN SOCIOLOGY Allen and Unwin London 1968

Moser C A and Scott W — BRITISH TOWNS: A STATISTICAL STUDY OF THEIR
SOCIAL AND ECNOMIC DIFFERENCES Oliver and
Boyd Edinburgh 1961

Pahl R ed — READINGS IN URBAN SOCIOLOGY Pergamon Oxford
1968

Taylor George and Ayres N — BORN, BRED UNEQUAL Longman London 1969

Weber A — THE GROWTH OF CITIES IN THE 19th CENTURY
Cornell University Press Ithaca New York
1963

Williams Raymond — THE COUNTRY AND THE CITY Chatto and Windus
London 1973

J 20   Internal migration

Donnison D V 'The movement of households in England' Journal of the Royal Statistical Society (series A) 124(1) 1961

Friedlander D and Roshier R J INTERNAL MIGRATION IN ENGLAND AND WALES 1851 to 1951 (reprinted from Population Studies 19(3) 20(1) March - July 1966) 1966

Harris A I and Clausen R LABOUR MOBILITY IN GREAT BRITAIN 1953-1963 UK Social Survey HMSO London 1967

Hill A B INTERNAL MIGRATION AND ITS EFFECTS UPON THE DEATH RATES (Medical Research Council Special Reports No 95) 1925

Hollingsworth T H MIGRATION: A STUDY BASED ON SCOTTISH EXPERIENCE BETWEEN 1939 and 1964 Oliver and Boyd Edinburgh 1971

Jackson J A ed 'Migration' Sociology Studies 2 Cambridge University Press London 1969

Newton M P and Jeffery J R INTERNAL MIGRATION (General Register Office Studies on Medical and Population Subjects No 5) HMSO London 1951

Ravenstein E G 'The laws of migration' Journal of the Statistical Society 48(2) June 1885; 52(2) June 1889
(see also: Thomas D S et al RESEARCH MEMORANDUM ON MIGRATION DIFFERENTIALS New York Social Science Research Council New York 1938)

Rowntree J A INTERNAL MIGRATION: A STUDY OF THE FREQUENCY OF MOVEMENT OF MIGRANTS (General Register Office Studies on Medical and Population Subjects No 11) London HMSO 1957

Welch Ruth L 'Migration in Britain: an appraisal of research findings' Greater London Council Bulletin 7

J 30   Urban concentration and diffusion

Centre for Urban Studies ed LONDON - ASPECTS OF CHANGE MacGibbon and Kee London 1964

Donnison David and Eversley David eds LONDON: URBAN PATTERNS, PROBLEMS AND POLICIES Heinemann London 1973

Freeman T W THE CONURBATIONS OF GREAT BRITAIN Manchester University Press Manchester 1966 (2nd ed)

Green L P	PROVINCIAL METROPOLIS: THE FUTURE OF LOCAL GOVERNMENT IN SOUTH-EAST LANCASHIRE Allen and Unwin London 1959
Jackson Alan	SEMI-DETACHED LONDON Allen and Unwin London 1973
Jones E and Sinclair D J eds	ATLAS OF LONDON AND THE LONDON REGION Pergamon Oxford 1969
Lawton R	'The daily journey to work in England and Wales' Town Planning Review 29(4) January 1959
Liepmann K	THE JOURNEY TO WORK Kegan Paul and Co London 1944
Pahl R E	URBS IN RURE: THE METROPOLITAN FRINGE IN HERT-FORDSHIRE London School of Economics (Geography Department) 1965
Pahl R E	WHOSE CITY? AND OTHER ESSAYS ON SOCIOLOGY AND PLANNING Longman London 1970
Pahl R E	PATTERNS OF URBAN LIFE Longman London 1970
Robson B T	URBAN ANALYSIS: A STUDY OF CITY STRUCTURE WITH SPECIAL REFERENCE TO SUNDERLAND Cambridge University Press Cambridge 1969
Rosing Kenneth E and Wood Peter A	CHARACTER OF A CONURBATION University of London Press London 1971
Thompson Eric J	'Analyses of census data for London' Greater London Council Bulletins 4 and 8
Thorns D C	SUBURBIA Macgibbon and Kee London 1972
Westergaard J H	'Journeys to work in the London region' Town Planning Review 28(1) April 1957 (see also Centre for Urban Studies London... above)
Wibberley G P	AGRICULTURE AND URBAN GROWTH Michael Joseph London 1960

J 40 Urban and regional planning

J 40 General

Ashworth W	THE GENESIS OF MODERN BRITISH TOWN PLANNING Routledge and Kegan Paul London 1954
Batley Richard	'An explanation of non-participation in planning' Policy and Politics vol 1 no 2 95-114 1971
Broady M	PLANNING FOR PEOPLE: ESSAYS ON THE SOCIAL CONTEXT OF PLANNING Bedford Square Press London 1968

Cameron Gordon C and Wingo Lowdon eds — CITIES REGIONS AND PUBLIC POLICY Oliver and Boyd Edinburgh 1973

Centre for Urban Studies — LAND USE PLANNING AND THE SOCIAL SCIENCES: A SELECTED BIBLIOGRAPHY C U S London 1964 and SUPPLEMENT 1970

Centre for Urban Studies ed — LONDON — ASPECTS OF CHANGE MacGibbon and Kee London 1964

Cherry Gordon E — URBAN CHANGE AND PLANNING: A HISTORY OF URBAN DEVELOPMENT IN BRITAIN SINCE 1750 G T Foulis London 1972

Cowan P et al — DEVELOPING PATTERNS OF URBANISATION Oliver and Boyd Edinburgh 1970

Cowan P ed — THE FUTURE OF PLANNING Heinemann London 1973

Cullingworth J B — HOUSING NEEDS AND PLANNING POLICY Routledge and Kegan Paul London 1960

Davies Jon Gower — THE EVANGELISTIC BUREAUCRAT: A STUDY OF A PLANNING EXERCISE IN NEWCASTLE UPON TYNE Tavistock London 1972

Dennis Norman — PUBLIC PARTICIPATION AND PLANNERS BLIGHT Faber London 1972

Dennis Norman — PEOPLE AND PLANNING Faber London 1970

Eversley David — THE PLANNER IN SOCIETY: THE CHANGING ROLE OF A PROFESSION Faber London 1973

Ferris John — PARTICIPATION IN URBAN PLANNING: THE BARNSBURY CASE, A STUDY OF ENVIRONMENTAL IMPROVEMENT IN LONDON Bell London 1972

Friend J K and Jessop W N — LOCAL GOVERNMENT AND STRATEGIC CHOICE Tavistock London 1969

Glass R — 'The evaluation of planning: some sociological considerations' International Social Science Journal 11(3) 1959 (see also Foley D L 'British Town planning: one ideology or three?' British Journal of Sociology 11(3) September 1960)

Hall Peter — LONDON 2000 Faber London 1963 (revised ed Faber 1970)

Hall Peter et al — THE CONTAINMENT OF URBAN ENGLAND Vol 1 Urban and Metropolitan Growth Processes Vol 2 The Planning System: Objectives, Operations and Impacts George Allen and Unwin London 1973

Hemming M F W   'The regional problem' National Institute of
                             Economics Review no 25 August 1963

McCrone Gavin   REGIONAL POLICY IN BRITAIN Allen and Unwin
                             London 1969

Reade E   'Some notes towards a sociology of planning –
                             the case for self-awareness' Journal of the
                             Town Planning Institute vol 54 1968

Stone P A   HOUSING TOWN DEVELOPMENT LAND AND COST Estates
                             Gazette London 1963

Stone P A   URBAN DEVELOPMENTS IN BRITAIN Cambridge Univer-
                             sity Press Cambridge 1970

Stone P A   THE STRUCTURE SIZE AND COST OF URBAN SETTLE-
                             MENT Cambridge University Press Cambridge 1973

United Kingdom: Royal   REPORT (cmnd 6153) 1940 (Barlow report)
Commission on the Dis-
tribution of the Indus-
trial Population

United Kingdom: Ministry   REPORT OF THE COMMITTEE ON LAND UTILISATION IN
of Works and Planning   RURAL AREAS (cmnd 6378) 1942 (Scott Report)

United Kingdom: Ministry   FINAL REPORT OF THE EXPERT COMMITTEE ON COMPEN-
of Works and Planning   SATION AND BETTERMENT (cmnd 6386) 1942 (Uthwatt
                             Report)

United Kingdom: Ministry   REPORT OF THE COMMITTEE ON THE QUALIFICATIONS
of Town and Country Plan-   OF PLANNERS (cmnd 8059) 1950 (Schuster Report)
ning

United Kingdom: People   REPORT OF THE COMMITTEE ON PUBLIC PARTICIPATION
and Planning   IN PLANNING (Skeffington Report) HMSO London
                             1969

Westergaard J H   'Land use planning since 1951: the legislative
                             and administrative framework in England and
                             Wales' Town Planning Review 35(3) October 1964

J 41 Decentralisation, New Towns, Neighbourhood Units

Benney M   'Storm over Stevenage' in Weidenfeld A G THE
                             CHANGING NATION Contact Books No 7 Contact
                             Publications London 1947

Dahir J   THE NEIGHBOURHOOD UNIT PLAN: ITS SPREAD AND
                             ACCEPTANCE Russell Sage Foundation New York
                             1947

Dennis N   'The popularity of the neighbourhood community
                             idea' Sociological Review 6(2) December 1958

Dunning J H   'Manufacturing industry in the New Towns' _Manchester School_ 28(2) May 1960

Foley D L   CONTROLLING LONDON'S GROWTH... 1940-1960 Cambridge University Press Cambridge 1963

Heraud B J   'Social class and the New Towns' _Urban Studies_ vol 5 1968

Howard E   GARDEN CITIES OF TOMORROW Swan Sonnenschein & Co London 1902 (1st ed 1898)

Mumford L   THE CITY IN HISTORY Secker and Warburg London 1961

Nicholson J H   NEW COMMUNITIES IN BRITAIN National Council of Social Service London 1961

Orlans H   STEVENAGE: A SOCIOLOGICAL STUDY OF A NEW TOWN Routledge and Kegan Paul London 1952

Rodwin L   THE BRITISH NEW TOWNS POLICY Oxford University Press Oxford 1956

Self P   CITIES IN FLOOD Faber London 1961 (1st ed 1957)

Thomas R   AYCLIFFE TO CUMBERNAULD: A STUDY OF SEVEN NEW TOWNS IN THEIR REGIONS (PEP broadsheets no 516) PEP London 1969

Thomas R   LONDON'S NEW TOWNS PEP London 1969

United Kingdom: Ministry of Town and Country Planning   NEW TOWNS COMMITTEE: FINAL REPORT (cmnd 6876) 1946 (Reith Committee) HMSO London

J 42 Social surveys for planning

Brennan T   MIDLAND CITY: WOLVERHAMPTON SOCIAL AND INDUSTRIAL SURVEY Dobson London 1948

Brennan T   RESHAPING A CITY House of Grant Glasgow 1959

Carey Lynnette and Mapes Roy   THE SOCIOLOGY OF PLANNING: A STUDY OF SOCIAL ACTIVITY ON NEW HOUSING ESTATES Batsford London 1972

Centre for Urban Studies ed   LONDON - ASPECTS OF CHANGE MacGibbon and Kee London 1964

Collison P   THE CUTTLESLOWE WALLS Faber London 1963

Durant R   WATLING: A SURVEY OF SOCIAL LIFE ON A NEW HOUSING ESTATE P S King & Son London 1939 (see also Pahl R E ed READINGS IN URBAN SOCIO-LOGY Pergamon Oxford 1969)

Glass R

THE SOCIAL BACKGROUND OF A PLAN: A STUDY OF MIDDLESBROUGH Routledge and Kegan Paul London 1948

Hare E H and Shaw G K

MENTAL HEALTH ON A NEW HOUSING ESTATE Oxford University Press London 1965

Jennings H

SOCIETIES IN THE MAKING: A STUDY OF DEVELOPMENT AND REDEVELOPMENT WITHIN A COUNTY BOROUGH Routledge and Kegan Paul London 1962

Jevons R and Madge J

HOUSING ESTATES: A STUDY OF BRISTOL CORPORATION POLICY AND PRACTICE BETWEEN THE WARS Bristol University Press Bristol 1946

Kuper L et al

LIVING IN TOWNS Cresset Press London 1963

Liverpool University: Dept of Social Science

SOCIAL ASPECTS OF A TOWN DEVELOPMENT PLAN: A STUDY OF THE COUNTY BOROUGH OF DUDLEY Liverpool University Press Liverpool 1951

M'Gonigle G C M and Kirby J

POVERTY AND PUBLIC HEALTH Gollancz London 1936 (chapter 7)

Mitchell G D et al

NEIGHBOURHOOD AND COMMUNITY: AN ENQUIRY INTO SOCIAL RELATIONSHIPS ON HOUSING ESTATES IN LIVERPOOL AND SHEFFIELD Liverpool University Press Liverpool 1955

Mogey J M

FAMILY AND NEIGHBOURHOOD: TWO STUDIES IN OXFORD Oxford University Press London 1956

Morris R N and Mogey J M

THE SOCIOLOGY OF HOUSING: STUDIES AT BERINSFIELD Routledge and Kegan Paul London 1965

Spencer J et al

STRESS AND RELEASE IN AN URBAN ESTATE Tavistock Publications London 1964

Taylor S Lord and Chave S

MENTAL HEALTH AND ENVIRONMENT Longmans London 1963

Vereker C et al

URBAN REDEVELOPMENT AND SOCIAL CHANGE: A STUDY OF SOCIAL CONDITIONS IN CENTRAL LIVERPOOL 1955-1956 Liverpool University Press Liverpool 1961

Williams N

POPULATION PROBLEMS OF NEW ESTATES, WITH SPECIAL REFERENCE TO NORRIS GREEN Liverpool University Press Liverpool 1939

Willmott P

THE EVOLUTION OF A COMMUNITY Routledge and Kegan Paul London 1963

Young T

BECONTREE AND DAGENHAM: THE STORY OF THE GROWTH OF A HOUSING ESTATE Becontree Social Survey Committee London 1934

106

J 50 Other urban social surveys and town portraits
(see also: B 21 Social conditions in 19th century towns and cities)

Barker T C and Harris J R   A MERSEYSIDE TOWN IN THE INDUSTRIAL REVOLUTION:
                             ST HELENS 1750-1900 Liverpool University Press
                             Liverpool 1954

Bell Colin and Newby Howard THE SOCIOLOGY OF COMMUNITY Frank Cass London
eds   1972

Bell Colin and Newby Howard COMMUNITY STUDIES Allen and Unwin London 1972

Bell Lady F   AT THE WORKS Edward Arnold London 1907 Nelson
                             London 1911

Booth C ed   LIFE AND LABOUR OF THE PEOPLE IN LONDON 1892-
                             1903 (17 vols) Macmillan London 1902-3
                             (see also Pfautz H W below)

Brennan T et al   STUDY OF SOCIAL CHANGE IN SOUTH-WEST WALES
                             Watts London 1954

Briggs A   VICTORIAN CITIES Penguin Harmondsworth 1963

Centre for Urban Studies   LONDON - ASPECTS OF CHANGE McGibbon and Kee
ed   London 1964

Chaloner W H   THE SOCIAL AND ECONOMIC DEVELOPMENT OF CREWE
                             1780-1923 Manchester University Press Manchester
                             1950

Dennis N et al   COAL IS OUR LIFE Eyre and Spottiswoode London
                             1957

Elias N and Scotson J   THE ESTABLISHED AND THE OUTSIDERS Frank Cass
                             London 1965

George M D   LONDON LIFE IN THE 18TH CENTURY Routledge and
                             Kegan Paul London 1930 (1st ed 1925)

Gilbert E W   BRIGHTON: OLD OCEAN'S BAUBLE Methuen London
                             1954

Gill C and Briggs A   HISTORY OF BIRMINGHAM (2 vols) Oxford University
                             Press London 1952

Glass R ed   THIRD LONDON SURVEY Publisher and date of pub-
                             lication to be announced

Godwin G   TOWN SWAMPS AND SOCIAL BRIDGES 1859

Gomme G L   LONDON IN THE REIGN OF VICTORIA 1837-1897
                             1898

Hollingshead J   RAGGED LONDON IN 1861 1861

Jones D C   THE SOCIAL SURVEY OF MERSEYSIDE (3 vols)
                             Liverpool University Press Liverpool 1934

Jones E   A SOCIAL GEOGRAPHY OF BELFAST Oxford University
                             Press London 1960

Kerr M   THE PEOPLE OF SHIP STREET Routledge and Kegan
                             Paul London 1958

Klein J   SAMPLES FROM ENGLISH CULTURES Routledge and
                             Kegan Paul London 1965

Lawton R and Cunningham C M MERSEYSIDE SOCIAL AND ECONOMIC STUDIES Longmans
eds   London 1971

London Congregational   THE BITTER CRY OF OUTCAST LONDON 1883
Union (Preston W C)

Mayhew H   LONDON LABOUR AND THE LONDON POOR (4 vols)
                             1861-62
                             (selections in Quennell P MAYHEW'S LONDON
                             William Kinher London 1951)

Mays J B   GROWING UP IN THE CITY Liverpool University
                             Press Liverpool 1954

Mitchell J Clyde ed   SOCIAL NETWORKS IN URBAN SITUATIONS Manchester
                             University Press Manchester 1969

Pfautz H W ed.   CHARLES BOOTH ON THE CITY: PHYSICAL PATTERN
                             AND SOCIAL STRUCTURE University of Chicago Press
                             Chicago 1967

Power E R   'The social structure of an English county town'
                             Sociological Review 29(4) October 1937

Rasmussen S E   LONDON: THE UNIQUE CITY Penguin Harmondsworth
                             1961 (1st English ed 1937)

Rex J A and Moore R   RACE, COMMUNITY AND CONFLICT Oxford University
                             Press London 1967

Rosser C and Harris C   THE FAMILY AND SOCIAL CHANGE Routledge and Kegan
                             Paul London 1965

Rowntree B S   POVERTY: A STUDY OF TOWN LIFE Longmans London
                             1922 (1st ed 1901)

Rowntree B S   POVERTY AND PROGRESS: A SECOND SOCIAL SURVEY
                             OF YORK Longmans London 1946 (1st ed 1941)

Sainsbury P   SUICIDE IN LONDON: AN ECOLOGICAL STUDY Chapman
                             and Hall London 1955

Smith H L ed   THE NEW SURVEY OF LONDON LIFE AND LABOUR 1930-
                             1935 (9 vols) London School of Economics
                             London 1930-1935

Stacey M   TRADITION AND CHANGE: A STUDY OF BANBURY
                            Oxford University Press London 1960

Summerson J   GEORGIAN LONDON Pleiades Books London 1945

Wilkinson E   THE TOWN THAT WAS MURDERED: THE LIFE-STORY
                            OF JARROW Gollancz London 1939

Willmott P and Young M   FAMILY AND CLASS IN A LONDON SUBURB Routledge
                            and Kegan Paul London 1960

Young M and Willmott P   FAMILY AND KINSHIP IN EAST LONDON Routledge
                            and Kegan Paul London 1957

Young M and Willmott P   THE SYMMETRICAL FAMILY Routledge and Kegan Paul
                            London 1973

J 60 Housing

Bowley M   HOUSING AND THE STATE 1919-1944 Allen and Unwin
                            London 1945

Centre for Urban Studies   HOUSING IN CAMDEN (Borough Council of Camden)
et al   Centre for Urban Studies London 1969

Cullingworth J B   HOUSING IN TRANSITION: A CASE STUDY... Heinemann
                            London 1963

Cullingworth J B   HOUSING NEEDS AND PLANNING POLICY Routledge and
                            Kegan Paul London 1960

Donnison D V   THE GOVERNMENT OF HOUSING Penguin Harmondsworth
                            1967

Donnison D V   HOUSING POLICY SINCE THE WAR Codicote Press
                            Welwyn Herts 1960

Donnison D V et al   HOUSING SINCE THE RENT ACT Codicote Press Welwyn
                            Herts 1961

Glass R and Davidson F G   'Housing structure and housing needs' Population
                            Studies 4(4) March 1951

Glass R and Westergaard   LONDON'S HOUSING NEEDS University College London
         J H   Centre for Urban Studies 1965

Glastonbury Bryan   HOMELESS NEAR A THOUSAND HOMES Allen and Unwin
                            London 1971

Greve John   PRIVATE LANDLORDS IN BRITAIN Bell London 1965

Greve John   LONDON'S HOMELESS Bell London 1964

Greve John Page Dilys and   HOMELESSNESS IN LONDON Chatto and Windus London
Greve Stella   1972
                                (see also DHSS, LBA. FINAL REPORT OF THE JOINT
                                WORKING PARTY ON 'HOMELESS IN LONDON' DHSS
                                London 1972)

Harloe Michael Issacharoff   THE ORGANISATION OF HOUSING: PUBLIC AND PRIVATE
Ruth Minns Richard   ENTERPRISE IN LONDON Heinemann London 1974

Needleman L   THE ECONOMICS OF HOUSING Staples Press London
                                1965

Nevitt A A   HOUSING, TAXATION AND SUBSIDIES Nelson London
                                1966

United Kingdom: Ministry   REPORT OF THE COMMITTEE ON HOUSING IN GREATER
of Housing and Local   LONDON (cmnd 2605) HMSO London 1965
Government

J 70 Rural communities
(see also B 22 Social conditions in 19th century: in rural places)

Ashby M K   JOSEPH ASHBY OF TYSOE: A STUDY OF ENGLISH
                                VILLAGE LIFE Cambridge University Press London
                                1961

Crichton R   COMMUTERS' VILLAGE: A STUDY OF COMMUNITY AND
                                COMMUTING IN BERKSHIRE David and Charles,
                                Newton Abbot 1964

Emmett I   A NORTH WALES VILLAGE Routledge and Kegan Paul
                                London 1964

Frankenberg R   VILLAGE ON THE BORDER Cohen and West London 1957

Littlejohn J   WESTRIGG: THE SOCIOLOGY OF A CHEVIOT PARISH
                                Routledge and Kegan Paul London 1963

Mogey J M   RURAL LIFE IN NORTHERN IRELAND Oxford University
                                Press London 1947

Pahl R E   URBS IN RURE: THE METROPOLITAN FRINGE IN HERTFORD-
                                SHIRE London School of Economics Geographical
                                Paper no 2 1965

Rees A D   LIFE IN A WELSH COUNTRYSIDE University of Wales
                                Press Cardiff 1950

Saville J   RURAL DEPOPULATION IN ENGLAND AND WALES 1851-
                                1951 Routledge and Kegan Paul London 1957

Williams W M   A WEST COUNTRY VILLAGE: ASHWORTHY Routledge and
                                Kegan Paul London 1963

Williams W M   THE SOCIOLOGY OF AN ENGLISH VILLAGE: GOSFORTH
                                Routledge and Kegan Paul London 1956

Dell S — SILENT IN COURT Occasional Papers in Social Administration Bell London 1971

Gibson E — TIME SPENT AWAITING TRIAL HMSO London 1960

Grunhut M — JUVENILE OFFENDERS BEFORE THE COURTS Clarendon Press Oxford 1956

Hepple B A — RACE JOBS AND THE LAW IN BRITAIN Penguin Harmondsworth 1970

Herman M — ADMINISTRATIVE JUSTICE AND SUPPLEMENTARY BENEFITS Occasional Papers in Social Administration Bell London 1972

Hood R — SENTENCING IN MAGISTRATE'S COURTS Stevens London 1962

Hood R — SENTENCING THE MOTORING OFFENDER Heinemann London 1972

"Justice" — CRIMINAL APPEALS Stevens London 1964

"Justice" — HOME OFFICE REVIEWS OF CRIMINAL CONVICTIONS Stevens London 1968

"Justice" — THE JUDICIARY Stevens London 1970

"Justice" — THE PROSECUTION PROCESS IN ENGLAND AND WALES Stevens London 1970

"Justice" — TRIAL OF MOTOR ACCIDENT CASES Stevens London 1966

King M and Jackson C — BAIL OR CUSTODY Cobden Trust London 1971

McCabe S and Purves R — BY-PASSING THE JURY Blackwell Oxford 1972

McCabe S and Purves R — THE JURY AT WORK: A STUDY OF A SERIES OF JURY TRIALS IN WHICH DEFENDANTS WERE ACQUITTED Blackwell Oxford 1972

Meggarry R E — LAWYERS AND LITIGANTS IN ENGLAND Stevens London 1962

Palmer T — THE TRIALS OF OZ Blond and Briggs London 1971

Patchett K W and McClean J D — 'Decision making in juvenile cases' Criminal Law Review 1965 pp 699

Paterson A — A REPORT ON LEGAL AID AS A SOCIAL SERVICE Cobden Trust London 1970

Softley P — A SURVEY OF FINE ENFORCEMENT HMSO London 1973

Tennant T G — 'The use of remand on bail or in custody by the London Juvenile Courts — a comparative study' <u>British Journal of Criminology</u> 11 1971

Thomas D A — PRINCIPLES OF SENTENCING Heinemann London 1970

United Kingdom — REPORT OF THE INTERDEPARTMENTAL COMMITTEE ON THE BUSINESS OF THE CRIMINAL COURTS (Streatfield Report) (cmnd 1289) HMSO London 1961

United Kingdom — THE SENTENCE OF THE COURT Heinemann London 1970

Wraith R E and Lamb G B — PUBLIC INQUIRIES AS AN INSTRUMENT OF GOVERNMENT Allen and Unwin London 1971

Zander M — 'Access to a solicitor in a police station' <u>Criminal Law Review</u> 1972 p 342

Zander M — 'A study of bail/custody decisions in London Magistrate's Courts' <u>Criminal Law Review</u> 1971 p 191

Zander M — LAWYERS AND THE PUBLIC INTEREST Weidenfeld and Nicolson London 1968

Zander M — 'The unrepresented defendent in the Criminal Courts' <u>Criminal Law Review</u> 1969 p 632

Zander M — 'Who goes to solicitors' <u>Law Society Gazette</u> 66 1969

K 20 Law enforcement: agencies of formal social control: the police

Banton M — THE POLICEMAN AND THE COMMUNITY Tavistock London 1964

Brooker G — RURAL DISORDER AND POLICE REFORM IN IRELAND 1812—1836 Routledge and Kegan Paul London 1970

Cain M E — SOCIETY AND THE POLICEMAN'S ROLE Routledge and Kegan Paul London 1973

Critchley T A — A HISTORY OF THE POLICE IN ENGLAND AND WALES Constable London 1967

Grigg M — THE CHALLENOR CASE Penguin Harmondsworth 1963

Lambert R — CRIME, POLICE AND RACE RELATIONS Oxford University Press London 1970

Laurie P — SCOTLAND YARD Penguin Harmondsworth 1972

Martin J P and Wilson G — THE POLICE: A STUDY IN MANPOWER Heinemann London 1969

Reynolds G W and Judge A   THE NIGHT THE POLICE WENT ON STRIKE Weidenfeld
and Nicolson London 1968

Silver A   'The demand for order in a civil society: a
review of some recent themes in the history
of urban crime police and riot' in Bordua D ed
THE POLICE: SIX SOCIOLOGICAL ESSAYS Wiley New
York 1967

Steer D   POLICE CAUTIONS: A STUDY IN THE EXERCISE OF
POLICE DISCRETION Blackwell Oxford 1970

United Kingdom: Royal   FINAL REPORT (cmnd 1728) HMSO London 1962
Commission on the Police

Whitaker B   THE POLICE Penguin Harmondsworth 1964

K 21 Agencies of formal social control: the penal system

Andry R   THE SHORT TERM PRISONER Tavistock London 1963

Bottomley A K   DECISIONS IN THE PENAL PROCESS Martin Robertson
London 1974

Bottoms A E and   CRIMINALS COMING OF AGE Heinemann London 1973
McClintock F H

Cohen S and Taylor L   PSYCHOLOGICAL SURVIVAL: THE EXPERIENCE OF LONG-
TERM IMPRISONMENT Penguin Harmondsworth 1972

Davies C   'Pre-trial imprisonment: a Liverpool study'
British Journal of Criminology 11 1971

Dunlop A B and McCabe S   YOUNG MEN IN DETENTION CENTRES Routledge and
Kegan Paul London 1965

Emery F E   FREEDOM AND JUSTICE WITHIN WALLS Tavistock
London 1970

Fox L   THE ENGLISH PRISON AND BORSTAL SYSTEM Routledge
and Kegan Paul London 1952

Grunhut M   PENAL REFORM Oxford University Press London
1948

Hall-Williams J E   THE ENGLISH PENAL SYSTEM IN TRANSITION
Butterworth London 1970

Halmos P ed   SOCIOLOGICAL STUDIES IN THE BRITISH PENAL
SERVICES Sociological Review Monograph no 9
Keele 1965

Hammond W H and Chayen E   PERSISTENT CRIMINALS HMSO London 1963

Hood R   BORSTAL REASSESSED Heinemann London 1965

Klare H J   ANATOMY OF PRISON Penguin Harmondsworth 1962

McClean D and Wood J C   CRIMINAL JUSTICE AND THE TREATMENT OF OFFENDERS
                                   Sweet and Maxwell London 1969

McClintock F H et al   ATTENDANCE CENTRES Macmillan London 1961

Martin J P and Webster D   THE SOCIAL CONSEQUENCES OF CONVICTION Heinemann
                                   London 1971

Morris T P and Morris P   PENTONVILLE: A SOCIOLOGICAL STUDY OF AN ENG-
                                   LISH PRISON Routledge and Kegan Paul London
                                   1963

Parker T   THE FRYING PAN: A PRISON AND ITS PRISONERS
                                   Hutchinson London 1970

Playfair G   THE PUNITIVE OBSESSION Gollancz London 1971

Rose G   SCHOOLS FOR YOUNG OFFENDERS Tavistock London
                                   1967

Smith A   WOMEN IN PRISON Stevens London 1962

Sparks R F   LOCAL PRISONS: THE CRISIS IN THE ENGLISH PENAL
                                   SYSTEM Heinemann London 1972

Thomas J E   THE ENGLISH PRISON OFFICER SINCE 1850 Rout-
                                   ledge and Kegan Paul London 1972

United Kingdom   ELEVENTH REPORT OF THE COMMON'S ESTIMATES
                                   COMMITTEE: PRISONS BORSTALS AND DETENTION
                                   CENTRES HMSO London 1967

United Kingdom   PENAL PRACTICE IN A CHANGING SOCIETY (cmnd
                                   645) HMSO London 1959

United Kingdom   PEOPLE IN PRISON (cmnd 4214) HMSO London 1969

United Kingdom   REPORT OF THE INQUIRY INTO PRISON ESCAPES
                                   AND SECURITY (The Mountbatten Report) (cmnd
                                   3175) HMSO London 1966

United Kingdom   THE ADULT OFFENDER (cmnd 2852) HMSO London
                                   1965

United Kingdom   THE ORGANISATION OF AFTER-CARE HMSO London
                                   1963

United Kingdom   THE REGIME FOR LONG TERM PRISONERS IN CONDI-
                                   TIONS OF MAXIMUM SECURITY report of the Ad-
                                   visory Council on the Penal System (The
                                   Radzinowicz Report) HMSO London 1968

United Kingdom	THE WAR AGAINST CRIME IN ENGLAND AND WALES 1959-64 (cmnd 2296) HMSO London 1964
West D J ed	THE FUTURE OF PAROLE Duckworth London 1972
West D J	THE HABITUAL OFFENDER Macmillan London 1963

K 22 Other agencies of formal social control

Barr H and O'Leary E	TRENDS AND REGIONAL COMPARISONS IN PROBATION HMSO London 1966
Carson W G	'Some sociological aspects of strict liability and the enforcement of factory legislation' Modern Law Review 33 1970
Davies M	PROBATIONERS IN THEIR SOCIAL ENVIRONMENT HMSO London 1969
Davies M	SOCIAL ENQUIRY REPORTS AND THE PROBATION SERVICE HMSO London 1973
Folkard S et al	PROBATION RESEARCH: A PRELIMINARY REPORT HMSO London 1966
Ford P	ADVISING SENTENCERS Blackwell Oxford 1972
Jarvis F V	'Inquiry before sentence' in Grygier T ed CRIMINOLOGY IN TRANSITION Tavistock London 1965
Morris P	PRISONERS AND THEIR FAMILIES Allen and Unwin London 1965
Morris P	PUT AWAY Routledge and Kegan Paul London 1969
Parsloe P	WORK OF THE PROBATION AND AFTER-CARE OFFICER Routledge and Kegan Paul London 1967
Rock P E	MAKING PEOPLE PAY Routledge and Kegan Paul London 1973
Seed P	THE EXPANSION OF SOCIAL WORK IN BRITAIN Routledge and Kegan Paul London 1973
Silberman M et al	EXPLORATIONS IN AFTER-CARE HMSO London 1971
Smith C et al	THE WINCROFT YOUTH PROJECT Tavistock London 1972
United Kingdom	FIRST REPORT OF THE EXPENDITURE COMMITTEE - PROBATION AND AFTER-CARE HMSO London 1972

K 30   Deviance

K 30   General

Arnott J E and Duncan J A	THE SCOTTISH CRIMINAL Edinburgh University Press Edinburgh 1970
Bottoms A E	'Delinquency amongst immigrants' Race 8 1967
Box S	DEVIANCE REALITY AND SOCIETY Holt Rinehart and Winston London 1971
Carson W G and Wiles P eds	CRIME AND DELINQUENCY IN BRITAIN: SOCIOLOGICAL READINGS Martin Robertson London (1st ed 1971 2nd ed 1975)
Chesney K	THE VICTORIAN UNDERWORLD Penguin Harmondsworth 1972
Cohen S ed	IMAGES OF DEVIANCE Penguin Harmondsworth 1971
Heidensohn F	'The deviance of women' British Sociological Journal 19 1960
Home Office Research Unit	REPORT NO 11: STUDIES OF FEMALE OFFENDERS HMSO London 1967
Jones H	CRIME AND THE PENAL SYSTEM University Tutorial Press London 1965
Linesmith A and Levin Y	'English Ecology and Criminology of the Past Century' Journal of Criminal Law Criminology and Police Science 6 1937
Little A	'The prevalence of recorded delinquency and recidivism in England and Wales' American Sociological Review 30 1965
McClintock F H and Avison N H	CRIME IN ENGLAND AND WALES Heinemann London 1968
Mannheim H	SOCIAL ASPECTS OF CRIME IN ENGLAND BETWEEN THE WARS Allen and Unwin London 1940
Mayo P E	THE MAKING OF A CRIMINAL Weidenfeld and Nicolson London 1964
Morris T P	THE CRIMINAL AREA Routledge and Kegan Paul London 1957
Rex J and Moore R	RACE COMMUNITY AND CONFLICT Oxford University Press London 1967
Shields J V M and Duncan J A	THE STATE OF CRIME IN SCOTLAND Tavistock London 1964

Spencer J — STRESS AND RELEASE IN AN URBAN ESTATE Tavistock London 1964

Taylor I and Taylor L eds — POLITICS AND DEVIANCE Penguin Harmondsworth 1973

Tobias J — CRIME AND INDUSTRIAL SOCIETY IN THE NINETEENTH CENTURY Batsford London 1967

United Kingdom — REPORT OF THE DEPARTMENTAL COMMITTEE ON CRIMINAL STATISTICS (Perk's Committee) (cmnd 3448) HMSO London 1968

Walker N — CRIME AND PUNISHMENT IN BRITAIN Edinburgh University Press Edinburgh 1968

Walker N — CRIMES, COURTS AND FIGURES Penguin Harmondsworth 1971

K 31   Juvenile delinquency and gangs

Bagley C — 'Juvenile delinquency in Exeter' Urban Studies 2 1965

Bagot J H — JUVENILE DELINQUENCY Jonathan Cape London 1941

Baldwin J — 'Delinquent Schools in Tower Hamlets: a critique' British Journal of Criminology 13 1972

Cohen P — 'Subcultural conflict and working class community' in WORKING PAPERS IN CULTURAL STUDIES University of Birmingham 1972

Cohen S — FOLK DEVILS AND MORAL PANICS: THE CREATION OF THE MODS AND ROCKERS Paladin London 1972

Daniel S and McGuire P eds — THE PAINTHOUSE: WORDS FROM AN EAST END GANG Penguin Harmondsworth 1972

Downes D — THE DELINQUENT SOLUTION Routledge and Kegan Paul London 1965

Ferguson T — THE YOUNG DELINQUENT IN HIS SOCIAL SETTING Oxford University Press London 1952

Mannheim H — JUVENILE DELINQUENCY IN AN ENGLISH MIDDLE TOWN Routledge and Kegan Paul London 1944

Mays J B — CRIME AND THE SOCIAL STRUCTURE Faber London 1967

Mays J B — GROWING UP IN THE CITY Liverpool University Press Liverpool 1954

Mays J B — ON THE THRESHOLD OF DELINQUENCY Liverpool University Press Liverpool 1959

Patrick J — A GLASGOW GANG OBSERVED Methuen London 1972

Phillipson M — 'Juvenile delinquency and the school' in Carson W G and Wiles P eds CRIME AND DELIN- QUENCY IN BRITAIN Martin Robertson London 1971

Power M J et al — 'Neighbourhood school and juveniles before the Court' British Journal of Criminology 12 1972

Power M J and Sirey E C — 'Commentary on "Delinquent Schools in Tower Hamlets"' British Journal of Criminology 12 1972

Rock P E and Cohen S — 'The Teddy Boys' in Bogdanor V and Skidelsky R eds THE AGE OF AFFLUENCE 1951-1964 Macmillan London 1970

Scott P D — 'Gangs and delinquent groups in London' British Journal of Delinquency 7 1956

Sugarman B — 'Involvement in youth culture academic achieve- ment and conformity in school' British Journal of Sociology 18 1967

Taylor L — 'Soccer consciousness and soccer hooliganism' in Cohen S ed IMAGES OF DEVIANCE Penguin Har- mondsworth 1971

Ward C ed — VANDALISM AND ARCHITECTURE Architectural Press London 1973

Willis P — 'The motorbike within a subcultural group' in Working Papers in Cultural Studies 2 University of Birmingham 1972

Willmott P — ADOLESCENT BOYS OF EAST LONDON Routledge and Kegan Paul London 1966

K 32   Delinquency and Social Class

Belson W A — 'The extent of stealing by London boys' Advancement of Science 25 no 124 December 1968

Douglas J W B et al — 'Delinquency and social class' British Journal of Criminology 6 1966

Little W R and Ntsekhe V R — 'Social class backgrounds of young offenders from London' British Journal of Criminology 10 1959

MacDonald L — SOCIAL CLASS AND DELINQUENCY Faber and Faber London 1969

Palmai G et al — 'Social class and the young offender' British Journal of Psychiatry 113 1967

K 33 Professional and organised crime

Greenwood C — FIREARMS CONTROL Forensic Science Society London 1967

McClintock F H and Gibson E — ROBBERY IN LONDON Macmillan London 1961

McIntosh M — 'Changes in the organisation of thieving' in Cohen S ed IMAGES OF DEVIANCE Penguin Harmondsworth 1971

Mack J — 'Full-time miscreants delinquent neighbourhoods and criminal network' British Journal of Criminology 4 1967

Mack J — 'The able criminal' British Journal of Criminology 12(1) January 1972

K 34 Homocide and violence

Gibson E and Klein S — MURDER HMSO London 1969

Legal Research Unit — CRIMINAL HOMICIDE IN ENGLAND AND WALES 1957–1968 Bedford College London 1969

McClintock F H et al — CRIMES OF VIOLENCE Macmillan London 1963

West D J — MURDER FOLLOWED BY SUICIDE Heinemann London 1965

K 35 Drugs

Archard P — 'Sad bad or mad: society's confused response to the Skid Row alcoholic' in Bailey R and Young J eds CONTEMPORARY SOCIAL PROBLEMS IN BRITAIN Saxon House Farnborough 1973

Auld J — 'Drug use: the mystification of accounts' in Bailey R and Young J eds CONTEMPORARY SOCIAL PROBLEMS IN BRITAIN Saxon House Farnborough 1973

Bean P — THE SOCIAL CONTROL OF DRUGS Martin Robertson London 1974

Glatt M M et al — THE DRUG SCENE IN GREAT BRITAIN Edward Arnold London 1967

Schofield M — THE STRANGE CASE OF POT Penguin Harmondsworth 1971

Schur E M — NARCOTIC ADDICTION IN BRITAIN AND AMERICA Indiana University Press 1962

United Kingdom: Advisory Committee on Drug Dependence — REPORT ON CANNABIS HMSO London 1968

Young J — 'Student drug use and middle class delinquency' in Bailey R and Young J eds CONTEMPORARY SOCIAL PROBLEMS IN BRITAIN Saxon House Farnborough 1973

Young J — THE DRUGTAKERS Paladin London 1971

K 36 Sexual deviance

Manson I and Palmer J — 'Moralists in the moron market' in Bailey R and Young J eds CONTEMPORARY SOCIAL PROBLEMS IN BRITAIN Saxon House Farnborough 1973

Montgomery-Hyde H — THE OTHER LOVE: A HISTORICAL AND CONTEMPORARY SURVEY OF HOMOSEXUALITY IN BRITAIN Heinemann London 1970

Pearce F and Roberts A — 'The social regulation of sexual behaviour and the development of industrial capitalism in Britain' in Bailey R and Joung J eds CONTEMPORARY SOCIAL PROBLEMS IN BRITAIN Saxon House Farnborough 1973

Plummer K — 'Awareness of homosexuality' in Bailey R and Young J eds CONTEMPORARY SOCIAL PROBLEMS IN BRITAIN Saxon House Farnborough 1973

Plummer K ed — DEVIANCE REALITY AND SEXUALITY Routledge and Kegan Paul London 1974

Radzinowicz L ed — SEXUAL OFFENCES Macmillan London 1957

Rolph C H ed — WOMEN OF THE STREETS Secker and Warburg London 1955

Schofield M — THE SEXUAL BEHAVIOUR OF YOUNG PEOPLE Longmans London 1965 (revised 1968)

Schofield M — THE SEXUAL BEHAVIOUR OF YOUNG ADULTS Allen Lane London 1973

Schofield M — SOCIOLOGICAL ASPECTS OF HOMOSEXUALITY Longmans London 1965

Taylor L — 'The significance and interpretation of replies to motivational questions: the case of sex offenders' Sociology 6 1972

K 37   Other deviance: general

Gibbens T C N and Prince J   SHOPLIFTING Institute for the study and treatment of delinquency London 1962

Hepworth M and Featherstone M   'Going missing' in Bailey R and Young J eds CONTEMPORARY SOCIAL PROBLEMS IN BRITAIN Saxon House Farnborough 1973

Hepworth M and Featherstone M   'Persons believed missing' in Rock P E and McIntosh M eds DEVIANCE AND SOCIAL CONTROL Tavistock London 1974

Martin J P   OFFENDERS AS EMPLOYEES Macmillan London 1962

Sainsbury P   SUICIDE IN LONDON Institute of Psychiatry London 1955

Willett T C   CRIMINAL ON THE ROAD Tavistock London 1964

Willett T C   DRIVERS AFTER SENTENCE Heinemann London 1973

L   CULTURE, LEISURE AND COMMUNICATION

L 10   Culture and leisure — general

Bocock Robert	RITUAL IN INDUSTRIAL SOCIETY: A SOCIOLOGICAL ANALYSIS OF RITUALISM IN MODERN ENGLAND Allen and Unwin London 1974
Durant H	THE PROBLEM OF LEISURE Routledge and Kegan Paul London 1938
Gorer G	DEATH, GRIEF AND MOURNING IN CONTEMPORARY BRITAIN Cresset Press London 1965
Hoggart Richard	THE USES OF LITERACY Penguin Harmondsworth 1955
Hoggart Richard	SPEAKING TO EACH OTHER vol I ABOUT SOCIETY vol II ABOUT LITERATURE Chatto and Windus London 1970
Klein J	SAMPLES FROM ENGLISH CULTURES Routledge and Kegan Paul London 1965
Leavis F R	MASS CIVILISATION AND MINORITY CULTURE Heffer Cambridge 1930
Lowenthal L and Lawson I	'The debate of cultural standards in 19th. century England' Social Research 30(4) Winter 1963
Murdock Graham	CULTURE CLASS AND SCHOOLING: THE IMPACT OF POP Constable London 1974
Nuttall Jeff	BOMB CULTURE Paladin London 1970
O'Higgins Paul	CENSORSHIP IN BRITAIN Nelson London 1972
Opie I and P	CHILDREN'S GAMES IN STREET AND PLAYGROUND Oxford University Press London 1969
Opie I and P	THE LORE AND LANGUAGE OF SCHOOL CHILDREN Oxford University Press London 1959
Roberts Kenneth	LEISURE Longmans London 1970
Smith Michael A Packer Stanley and Smith Cyril S eds	LEISURE AND SOCIETY IN BRITAIN Allen Lane London 1973
Thompson D ed	DISCRIMINATION AND POPULAR CULTURE Penguin Harmondsworth 1964 (2nd ed 1974)
Williams R	CULTURE AND SOCIETY Chatto and Windus London 1958
Williams R	THE LONG REVOLUTION Chatto and Windus London 1961

L 20   The mass media — general

Blumer Jay G and Ewbank Alison J
'Trade unionists, the mass media and unofficial strikes' British Journal of Industrial Relations March 1970

Cauter T and Downham J S
THE COMMUNICATION OF IDEAS Chatto and Windus London 1954

Halloran J Elliott P and Murdock G
DEMONSTRATIONS AND COMMUNICATION: A CASE STUDY Penguin Harmondsworth 1970

Hartmann Paul and Husband Charles
RACISM AND THE MASS MEDIA Davis—Poynter London 1974

McInnes C
ENGLAND, HALF ENGLISH MacGibbon and Kee London 1961

McQuail D
TOWARDS A SOCIOLOGY OF MASS COMMUNICATION Collier—Macmillan London 1969

Murdock G and Golding P
'For a Political Economy of Mass Communications' in Miliband R and Saville J eds THE SOCIALIST REGISTER 1973 Merlin Press London 1973

Seymour—Ure Colin
THE POLITICAL IMPACT OF MASS MEDIA Constable London 1974

Sociological Review Monograph
No 13 1969 on sociological aspects of mass communications

Tunstall Jeremy
THE ADVERTISING MAN IN LONDON ADVERTISING AGENCIES Chapman and Hall London 1964

Tunstall Jeremy
THE WESTMINSTER LOBBY CORRESPONDENTS: A SOCIOLOGICAL STUDY OF NATIONAL POLITICAL JOURNALISM Routledge and Kegan Paul London 1970

Tunstall Jeremy ed
MEDIA SOCIOLOGY Constable London 1970

Tunstall Jeremy
JOURNALISTS AT WORK: SPECIALIST CORRESPONDENTS: THEIR NEWS ORGANISATIONS NEWS SOURCES AND COMPETITOR—COLLEAGUES Constable London 1971

Unesco
WORLD COMMUNICATIONS 1964

Williams R
BRITAIN IN THE SIXTIES: COMMUNICATIONS Penguin Harmondsworth 1962

Williams R
COMMUNICATIONS Chatto and Windus London 1966 (revised ed)

L 21 The press literature and reading habits

Adburgham Alison — WOMEN IN PRINT: WRITING WOMEN AND WOMEN'S MAGA-ZINES FROM THE RESTORATION TO THE ACCESSION OF VICTORIA Allen and Unwin London 1972

Altick R D — THE ENGLISH COMMON READER Cambridge University Press London 1957

Aspinall A — POLITICS AND THE PRESS 1780-1850 Home and Van Thal London 1949

Ayerst David — GUARDIAN: BIOGRAPHY OF A NEWSPAPER Collins London 1971

Bagley Christopher — 'Race relations and the press: an empirical analysis' Race XV no 1 July 1973

Beavan J — THE PRESS AND THE PUBLIC (Fabian Tracts no 338) Fabian Society London 1962

Boston Richard ed — THE PRESS WE DESERVE Routledge and Kegan Paul London 1970

Bradbury Malcolm — THE SOCIAL CONTEXT OF MODERN ENGLISH LITERATURE Blackwell Oxford 1971

Camrose Viscount (Berry W E) — BRITISH NEWSPAPERS AND THEIR CONTROLLERS Cassell London 1947

Cohen Stanley and Young Jock — THE MANUFACTURE OF NEWS: DEVIANCE SOCIAL PROBLEMS AND THE MASS MEDIA Constable London 1973

Colquhoun I — A PROSPEROUS PRESS (Hobart Papers) Barrie and Rockliff London 1961

Cox C B and Dyson A E eds — THE TWENTIETH CENTURY MIND: HISTORY IDEAS AND LITERATURE IN BRITAIN vol 2 1918-1945 Oxford University Press London 1972

Craig David — THE REAL FOUNDATIONS: LITERATURE AND SOCIAL CHANGE Chatto and Windus London 1973

Cruse A — THE ENGLISHMAN AND HIS BOOKS IN THE EARLY 19TH CENTURY Harrap London 1930

Cudlipp H — PUBLISH AND BE DAMNED Dakers London 1953

Cudlipp H — AT YOUR PERIL Weidenfeld and Nicolson London 1962

Dalziel M — POPULAR FICTION A HUNDRED YEARS AGO Cohen and West London 1957

Economist Intelligence Unit — SURVEY OF THE NATIONAL NEWSPAPER INDUSTRY Economist Intelligence Unit London 1966

General Council of the Press REPORTS published annually

Gollin A   THE OBSERVER AND J L GARVIN Oxford University
                                  Press London 1960

Hambro C   NEWSPAPER LORDS IN BRITISH POLITICS Macdonalds
                                  London 1958

Herd H   THE MARCH OF JOURNALISM Allen and Unwin Lon-
                                  don 1952

Institute of Incorporated   NATIONAL READERSHIP SURVEY Institute of Incor-
Practitioners in Adverti-   porated Practitioners in Advertising London
sing   1954

Jackson Ian   THE PROVINCIAL PRESS AND THE COMMUNITY Man-
                                  chester University Press Manchester 1971

Kaldor N and Silverman R   A STATISTICAL ANALYSIS OF ADVERTISING EXPEN-
                                  DITURE AND THE REVENUE OF THE PRESS (N I E S R)
                                  Cambridge University Press London 1948

Lane Michael   'Publishing Managers Publishing House Organi-
                                  sation and Role Conflict' Sociology vol 4 no 3
                                  September 1970

Laurenson Diana T and   THE SOCIOLOGY OF LITERATURE MacGibbon and Kee
Swingewood Alan   London 1972

Leavis Q D   FICTION AND THE READING PUBLIC Chatto and
                                  Windus London 1932

Levy H P   THE PRESS COUNCIL Macmillan London 1967

Lewis John   THE LEFT BOOK CLUB: AN HISTORICAL RECORD
                                  Gollancz London 1970

Mass Observation   THE PRESS AND ITS READERS Prepared for the
                                  Advertising Service Guild, published by Art
                                  and Technics London 1949

Political and Economic   'Balance Sheet of the press' Planning 1955
Planning (PEP)   'Ownership of the press' Planning 1955
                                  'What's in the papers?' Planning 1957

Read D   PRESS AND PEOPLE 1790-1850 Edward Arnold Lon-
                                  don 1960

Taylor H A   THE BRITISH PRESS Barker London 1961

Thomson P   THE VICTORIAN HEROINE: A CHANGING IDEAL 1837-
                                  1873 Oxford University Press London 1956

Times Publishing Company   THE HISTORY OF THE TIMES (4 vols) 1935-48

United Kingdom: Royal   REPORT HMSO London 1949
Commission on the Press

United Kingdom: Royal   REPORT (cmnd 7700) HMSO London 1962
Commission on the Press

Webb R K   'The Victorian reading public' in Ford B ed
                               FROM DICKENS TO HARDY Penguin Harmondsworth
                               1958

White Cynthia E   WOMEN'S MAGAZINES 1693-1968 Michael Joseph
                               London 1970

Williams F   DANGEROUS ESTATE: THE ANATOMY OF NEWSPAPERS
                               Longmans London 1957

Williams Raymond   THE ENGLISH NOVEL FROM DICKENS TO LAWRENCE
                               Chatto and Windus London 1970

L 22 Broadcasting cinema and music

Altmand W et al   T V: FROM MONOPOLY TO COMPETITION AND BACK?
                               Institute of Economic Affairs London 1962

Bakewell Joan and Garnham   THE NEW PRIESTHOOD Allen Lane London 1970
Nicholas eds

Belson W A   THE IMPACT OF TELEVISION Lockwood London 1967

Briggs A   HISTORY OF BROADCASTING vol 1 1961 vol 2 1965
                               vol 3 1970 Oxford University Press London

Crozier M   BROADCASTING: SOUND AND TELEVISION Oxford
                               University Press London 1958

Elliott Philip   THE MAKING OF A TELEVISION SERIES: A CASE
                               STUDY IN THE SOCIOLOGY OF CULTURE Constable
                               London 1972

Halloran James ed   THE EFFECTS OF TELEVISION Panther London 1970

Halloran James Brown R L   TELEVISION AND DELINQUENCY Leicester University
and Chaney D C   Press Leicester 1970

Hewatt Tim ed   ROLLING STONES FILE Panther London 1967

Jenkins C   THE POWER BEHIND THE SCREEN MacGibbon and Kee
                               London 1961

Newton F   THE JAZZ SCENE Penguin Harmondsworth 1961
                               (1st ed 1959)

Paulu B   BRITISH BROADCASTING Oxford University Press
                               London 1956

Paulu B   BRITISH BROADCASTING IN TRANSITION Macmillan
                               London 1961

Political and Economic   'Television in Britain' Planning 1958
Planning (PEP)

Simon of Wythenshawe (Lord) THE BBC FROM WITHIN Gollancz London 1953

Smith Anthony   THE SHADOW IN THE CAVE: THE BROADCASTER THE
                            AUDIENCE AND THE STATE Allen and Unwin London
                            1973

Trenaman J M and McQuail D TELEVISION AND THE POLITICAL IMAGE Methuen
                            London 1961

United Kingdom: Postmaster REPORT OF THE BROADCASTING COMMITTEES 1949
General   (cmnd 8116) HMSO London 1951
                            Also APPENDIX H (cmnd 8117) HMSO London 1951

United Kingdom: Postmaster REPORT OF THE COMMITTEE ON BROADCASTING 1960
General   (cmnd 1753) (Pilkington Committee) HMSO
                            London 1962

Wedell E G ed   STRUCTURES OF BROADCASTING Manchester Univer-
                            sity Press Manchester 1970

Williams Raymond   TELEVISION: TECHNOLOGY AND CULTURAL FORM
                            Fontana London 1974

Wilson H H   PRESSURE GROUP: THE CAMPAIGN FOR COMMERCIAL
                            TELEVISION Secker and Warburg London 1961

L 30 Sport and other recreation

Do nes D M et al   GAMBLING WORK AND LEISURE Routledge and Kegan
                            Paul London 1974

Dunning Eric ed   THE SOCIOLOGY OF SPORT Frank Cass London 1972

Mangan J A ed   PHYSICAL EDUCATION AND SPORT: SOCIOLOGICAL
                            AND CULTURAL PERSPECTIVES Blackwell Oxford 1973

Newman Otto   GAMBLING: HAZARD AND REWARD The Athlone Press
                            London 1972

Rust Frances   DANCE IN SOCIETY: AN ANALYSIS OF THE RELATION-
                            SHIP BETWEEN THE SOCIAL DANCE AND SOCIETY IN
                            ENGLAND FROM THE MIDDLE AGES TO THE PRESENT
                            DAY Routledge and Kegan Paul London 1969

M RELIGION
(see also B 41 Religion in the mid-nineteenth century)

M 10 General

ABC Television	TELEVISION AND RELIGION University of London Press London 1965
Brothers J	CHURCH AND SCHOOL Liverpool University Press Liverpool 1964
Brothers J	RELIGIOUS INSTITUTIONS Longmans Harlow 1971
Budd S	SOCIOLOGISTS AND RELIGION Collier-Macmillan 1973
Busia K	URBAN CHURCHES IN BRITAIN Lutterworth Press Woking 1966
Campbell C	TOWARDS A SOCIOLOGY OF IRRELIGION Macmillan London 1971
Day J D	THE GEOGRAPHY OF RELIGION IN ENGLAND Duckworth London 1971
Highet J	THE SCOTTISH CHURCHES Skeffington London 1960
Highet J	'Scottish religious adherence' British Journal of Sociology June 1962
Hill M	A SOCIOLOGY OF RELIGION Heinemann London 1973
Hill M	THE RELIGIOUS ORDER Heinemann London 1973
Inglis K S	CHURCHES AND THE WORKING CLASSES IN VICTORIAN ENGLAND Routledge and Kegan Paul London 1963
Independent Television Authority	RELIGION IN BRITAIN AND NORTHERN IRELAND ITA Publishing London 1970
Martin D A	PACIFISM: AN HISTORICAL AND SOCIOLOGICAL STUDY Routledge and Kegan Paul London 1965
Martin D A	A SOCIOLOGY OF ENGLISH RELIGION Heinemann London 1967
Martin D A ed	A SOCIOLOGICAL YEARBOOK OF RELIGION IN BRITAIN vol 1 1968 vol 2 1969 SCM Press London
Martin D A and Hill M eds	A SOCIOLOGICAL YEARBOOK OF RELIGION IN BRITAIN vol 3 1970 vol 4 1971 SCM Press London
Hill M ed	A SOCIOLOGICAL YEARBOOK OF RELIGION IN BRITAIN vol 5 1972 vol 6 1973 vol 7 1974 SCM Press London
MASS OBSERVATION	PUZZLED PEOPLE: A STUDY OF POPULAR ATTITUDES TO RELIGION Gollancz London 1948

Nicholls D	CHURCH AND STATE IN BRITAIN SINCE 1820 Routledge and Kegan Paul London 1967
Pickering W S F	'The persistence of Rites of Passage; an explanation' British Journal of Sociology 25(1) March 1974
Robertson R	THE SOCIOLOGICAL INTERPRETATION OF RELIGION Blackwell Oxford 1970
Robertson R	SOCIOLOGY OF RELIGION: SELECTED READINGS Penguin Harmondsworth 1969
Scharf B	THE SOCIOLOGICAL STUDY OF RELIGION Hutchinson London 1970
Spinks G S	RELIGION IN BRITAIN SINCE 1900 Dakers London 1962
Wickham E R	CHURCH AND PEOPLE IN AN INDUSTRIAL CITY Lutterworth Press Woking 1957
Zahn Gordon	CHAPLAINS IN THE RAF Manchester University Press Manchester 1969

M 20 Secularisation

Forster Peter G	'Secularisation in the English context: some conceptual and empirical problems' Sociological Review 20(2) May 1972
Macintyre A	SECULARISATION AND MORAL CHANGE Oxford University Press London 1967
Martin D A	THE RELIGIOUS AND THE SECULAR: STUDIES IN SECULARISATION Routledge and Kegan Paul London 1969
Pinder R	'Religious change in the process of secularisation' Sociological Review 19(3) August 1971
Wilson B	RELIGION IN SECULAR SOCIETY Watts London 1966

M 30 Anglicanism

Church Information Office	FACTS AND FIGURES ABOUT THE CHURCH OF ENGLAND 1962 1965 1968
Church Information Office	CHURCH OF ENGLAND YEARBOOK annually from 1968
Church Information Office	CHURCH AND STATE 1970

Coxon A P M — 'The Anglican Clergy' Sociology 1(1) 1967

Ferris P — THE CHURCH OF ENGLAND Gollancz London 1962 (revised ed Penguin Harmondsworth 1964)

Lloyd R — THE CHURCH OF ENGLAND 1900-1965 SCM Press London 1966

Morgan D H J — 'The social and educational background of anglican bishops' British Journal of Sociology 20(3) September 1969

Paul L — THE DEPLOYMENT AND PAYMENT OF THE CLERGY Church Information Office London 1964

Rudge P — MINISTRY AND MANAGEMENT Tavistock London 1968

Thompson Kenneth A — BUREAUCRACY AND CHURCH REFORM Clarendon Press Oxford 1970

Thompson R H T — THE CHURCH'S UNDERSTANDING OF ITSELF SCM Press London 1957

Towler R — 'The social status of the anglican minister' in Robertson R ed SOCIOLOGY OF RELIGION: SELECTED READINGS Penguin Harmondsworth 1969

Wagner D O — THE CHURCH OF ENGLAND AND SOCIAL REFORM SINCE 1854 Columbia University Press New York 1930

M 31 Methodism and nonconformity

Cowherd B — THE POLITICS OF ENGLISH DISSENT Epworth Press London 1959

Currie R — METHODISM DIVIDED Faber and Faber London 1968

Driver C — A FUTURE FOR THE FREE CHURCHES SCM Press London 1962

Semmel Bernard — THE METHODIST REVOLUTION Heinemann London 1974

Wearmouth R F — METHODISM AND THE TRADE UNIONS Epworth Press London 1959

Wearmouth R F — METHODISM AND THE STRUGGLE OF THE WORKING CLASSES 1850-1900 Backus Leicester 1954

Wearmouth R F — THE SOCIAL AND POLITICAL INFLUENCE OF METHODISM IN THE TWENTIETH CENTURY Epworth Press London 1957

M 32 Catholics and Jews
(see also I 30 Jews in Britain)

Beck G A   THE ENGLISH CATHOLICS 1850-1950 Burnes and
                                  Oates London 1950

Catholic Directory   Burnes and Oates annually

Gould J and Esh S   JEWISH LIFE IN MODERN BRITAIN Routledge and
                                  Kegan Paul London 1964

Ward C K   PRIESTS AND PEOPLE Liverpool University Press
                                  Liverpool 1961

M 33 Religious sects

Calley M J C   GOD'S PEOPLE Oxford University Press London
                                  1965

Nelson G K   SPIRITUALISM AND SOCIETY Routledge and Kegan
                                  Paul London 1969

Walker Andrew G and   'An Easter Pentecostal Convention: Management
Atherton James S   of a "Time of Blessing"' Sociological Review
                                  19(3) August 1971

Wilson B R ed   PATTERNS OF SECTARIANISM: ORGANISATION AND
                                  IDEOLOGY IN SOCIAL AND RELIGIOUS MOVEMENTS
                                  Heinemann London 1968

Wilson B   SECTS AND SOCIETY Heinemann London 1961

Wilson B   RELIGIOUS SECTS Weidenfeld and Nicolson London
                                  1970

Wildwood House

Post Industrial Society: by Alain Touraine (translated by Leonard F.X. Mayhew)

Is conflict any longer between the capitalist class and the workers or is it now mainly between technocracy and the people?
     William Cooper says in the *Sunday Times*: '. . . the book is held together by an integrated view of the way society is evolving, arrived at by a mind of strong and sustained analytic power. Add to that a strong predictive element — and you have a book which keeps making you break off reading to think.' Hardback £3.50 Paperback £1.50.

Beyond the Punitive Society: Operant Conditioning; Social and Political Aspects. Edited by Harvey Wheeler

Beyond the Punitive Society considers operant conditioning as a social technology and subjects it to technological assessment. This is truly a unique book, one that will find use in a wide variety at courses in psychology, political science, sociology, philosophy, policy studies and other fields. Hardback £3.25 Paperback £1.60.

Rules For Radicals: A Pragmatic Primer for Realistic Radicals and **Reveille For Radicals:** by Saul Alinsky

Saul Alinsky's work in organising the poor to fight for their rights has long been internationally famous. The books are his message, his prescription for direct actional organization and tactics. Both are essential for all activists bent on working for greater social and political justice.
Rules
Rules £0.90 *Reveille* £0.75.

The Technological Society: by Jacques Ellul

'Searching, incisive, ruthless analysis of the impact of technology on society and of the changes that are in consequence taking place . . . a major book of our times. Its prose is as lucid as its thought.'—*Nature.* Paperback £1.00.

The Learning Child: by Dorothy H. Cohen

This is a relevant guide to child development (in the years from five to eleven) intended especially for parents who worry about how their children learn at school and for all people who care how children feel as they learn. Hardback £3.00 Paperback £1.50.

Behaviour: The Control of Perception: by William Powers

This book, writes Paul J. Bohannan 'gives social scientists — an alternative to both behaviourism and psychoanalysis. It allows us to bring the soma, culture, society, behaviour, and experience into a single framework. We now know much more than we did before this book was published.' Hardback £5.50.

Post Scarcity Anarchism: by Murray Bookchin

Articles and essays from the pen of a New York anarchist, editor of *Anarchos* magazine; they include 'The Forms of Freedom', Towards a Liberatory Technology', 'Ecology and Revolutionary Thought', and 'Listen Marxists'. Although Boochin praises the 'conventional' counter culture he believes that it will transform society only when its concerns are wedded to libertarian theory. Hardback £2.95 Paperback £1.50.

When Reason Fails: by Robert A. Liston

When Reason Fails is a cogent and coherent attempt to make the theories and practics of psychotherapy understandable to everybody. Robert Liston brilliantly elucidates the field and the vocabulary and surveys the major theories and therapies. Hardback £2.50 Paperback £1.50.

Some Books by Paul Goodman

Communitas Means of Livelihood and Ways of Life Paperback £0.90
Growing Up Absurd Problems of Youth in the Organised System Paperback £0.90
People of Personnel Decentralising and the Mixed Systems Paperback £0.90

Roger Barnard writes in *New Society*:
     'Whether he wrote as a poet and novelist, as a political journalist or literary critic, there was an orgency, a broad humanism and moral passion to his work that made most other socially informed writings seem banal and lifeless in comparison.'

WILDWOOD HOUSE
1 Wardour Street
London W 1

SOCIOLOGY FROM ROUTLEDGE

DISCOVERING SOCIOLOGY
JOHN REX

Studies in Sociological Theory and Method   £3.75

HUMAN SOCIETIES
An Introduction to Sociology

GEOFFREY HURD

'It deserves to be extensively used in schools and colleges of education
and elsewhere not only as an introduction to sociology but as a basis for
the many courses that now draw on the subject ... Solid stuff and highly
recommended'. - Marten Shipman, *The Times Educational Supplement*
£2.95, paper £1.30

POOR PARENTS
Social Policy and the 'Cycle of Deprivation'

BILL JORDAN

A critique of official policy towards poor parents which looks in detail at
some of the myths prevalent in public debate - both political and academic -
about the 'cycle'.   £3.50, paper £1.75

PAUPERS
The Making of the New Claiming Class

BILL JORDAN

'It's a book which is essentially directed at the poor themsleves and it
outlines a militant scenario for the emergence of a poor people's movement
spearheaded by claimant's unions.' - Richard Beyant, *Social Service Quarterly*
£1.60, paper 80p

THE FAMILY AND SOCIAL CHANGE
COLIN ROSSER and CHRISTOPHER HARRIS

A Study of Family and Kinship in a South Wales Town   £4.25
International Library of Sociology

SOCIAL CLASS AND THE COMPREHENSIVE SCHOOL
JULIENNE FORD

'Readers of *New Society* will already be familiar with the import of this
study: that the social and educational objectives of the comprehensive school
have not been realised in practice.' - *New Society*   £2.25, paper £1.00

DICTIONARY OF SOCIOLOGY
EDITED BY G. DUNCAN MITCHELL

Designed especially to meet the needs of beginners in the study of sociology particularly students in universities and colleges who need a compact
one volume reference work.   £2.00, paper 90p

YOUTH AND THE SOCIAL ORDER
FRANK MUSGROVE

Deals with the status of Youth and the unequal conflict between the
generations; it is concerned with the strategy - and arrogance - of
the mature in protecting their position.   £1.75, paper £1.00

ROUTLEDGE & KEGAN PAUL
68-74 Carter Lane
London EC4V 5EL

FRANCES PINTER

TO BE AN ARAB IN ISRAEL
By Fouzi El-Asmar

Introduction by I.F. Stone
Preface by Uri Davis

The emergence of the Israeli Jewish state completely disrupted the lives of the Palestinian Arabs. Those remaining in Israel became a forgotten minority. Today the Arabs in Israel can no longer be treated as an invisible people. Fouzi El-Asmar tells of the impact of war on both Arabs and Jews, and provides important insights into the psychological disposition of the two communities towards each other. From his life story as poet, journalist, publisher and political prisoner, we are presented with a rarely seen portrayal of the Israeli way of life. He is critical of the political and social structures which perpetuate an exclusively Jewish state, but retains faith in the possibility of a truly binational secular state.

Fouzi El-Asmar was born in Haifa in 1937. As a journalist he has written for many newspapers and his poetry has been published in many countries. £1.95 paperback £5.00 hardback.

BRITISH THINKING ABOUT NUCLEAR WEAPONS
A.R.J. Groom: University College, London

British Thinking About Nuclear Weapons is a comprehensive study of governments, parties and pressure groups. On an issue which is fundamental to Britain's attempt to come to terms with the nuclear world and its role as a medium power, this book shows how a strategic issue raised basic questions in both domestic and foreign policy. Hardback £9.75.

WAR WITHOUT WEAPONS: NONVIOLENCE IN NATIONAL DEFENCE
Anders Boserup, University of Copenhagen, and Andrew Mack: Richardson Institute for Conflict and Peace Research, London

This study represents the first full length assessment of the existing literature. The various tactical options of non-violent strategy are integrated into an overall strategic theory. The more general issue of defence in the nuclear age is raised and it is shown that guerrilla warfare and non-military defence may, despite their manifest differences, be integrated into the framework of classical (Clausewitzian) strategic thinking. As such, both provide coherent, logical—but not of course unproblematic—strategies with which to confront a nuclear power. It is argued that only with the deployment of such strategies can the nuclear strategic dilemma of 'suicide or surrender' be avoided. As in all true strategy this is not achieved by futile appeals for disarmament but rather by imposing on the enemy one's own choice of weapons. Hardback £4.50 Softback £1.80.

GUERRILLA STRUGGLE IN AFRICA: AN ANALYSIS AND PREVIEW
Kenneth W. Grundy: Case Western Reserve University

Guerrilla Struggle in Africa is both a vital reference book for all concerned with the study of Africa, and an introduction to what the world can expect from this continent. It also makes a valuable contribution to the field of strategy.

... 'It has the virtue of collecting inside a single cover more hard data on both the theory and practice of guerrilla warfare in Africa than can be found elsewhere.'—*Africa Today*. A World Order Book. A Grossman book brought to you by Frances Pinter. Paperback £2.40.

FROM CITIZEN TO REFUGEE: UGANDA ASIANS COME TO BRITAIN
Mahmood Mamdani: University of Dar Es Salaam, Tanzania

Written by a Uganda Asian refugee, the author weaves his own life story into a thought-provoking analysis of the historical forces which shaped the present world structure. The 'divide and rule' tactics of the British colonialists are examined and discussed in terms of the resulting social positions held by the various tribes and races in Uganda today. The strategy of Amin is assessed in a cool analytical style rather than with the hysteria which dominated the news media at the time of the expulsion.

After explaining the causes and circumstances of the expulsion, Mahmood Mamdani turns to Britain, where he and 28,000 other Asians arrived during the winter of 1972. The process of resettlement was a hard one wrought with numerous problems. The Asians soon found that colour had a different significance in England than in Uganda; but that the result was simply another form of racism. Paperback £0.70.